Feedback for Banking Analytics: How to Survive and Thrive

"A deeply insightful book based on decades of experience. It really covers all you need to think about when approaching your analytics journey. At the core, it's not the technology. It's about the behaviours of the users of analytics and the consumers they are studying."
Joel Kornreich, Group CEO Alliance Bank Malaysia Berhad

"This step-by-step practical guide should be required reading for all senior managers and analytics practitioners looking to unlock customer value by making sense of the large volume of data they hold. It is THE essential guide to business analytics. Period."
Ernest Leung, Group COO, WeLab

"George lays out a comprehensive range of practical examples to guide readers on how to maximise customer and portfolio value. If you want to understand what works and what doesn't, then this is the book for you."
Shirley Wong,
General Manager and Head of Personal Banking, Bank of East Asia

"An exhaustive and insightful look at analytics for financial services. A work of enormous scope that demonstrates George's experience and expertise."
Denise Au-Yeung, CEO CXA Hong Kong

"I've been a CEO and board member for much of the last 20+ years. If this book had been around while I was in those roles, I would have ordered a copy for every Director and member of my exec team and told them it was a must read!"
Ian Marsh,
Former MD Asia Pacific Western Union and President/CEO Amex Japan

"George's gift is his ability to identify where and how to successfully apply analytics—extracting the maximum value for customers and increasing ROI. At last, he's committed some of that experience to print, condensing 35 years into 200 or so pages. If you can't get George to work with you, get the next best thing... read this book."
Abeed Rhemtulla, MD Enigma Group

Banking Analytics:
How to Survive and Thrive

George M. Haylett

Paperback ISBN: 9798579544902

Hardback ISBN: 9781838434007

Cover design and artwork: Book Design Stars

For Shirley,

Who makes everything worth it

*And for Nikki, Robert, Emmanuel, Marc and
the many others who actually did the work*

CONTENTS

Preface

Big Data and Analytics are officially sexy. It's true, everyone keeps telling us so. All banks should strive to become the next Google, Amazon, or some other perceived paragon in using data. Apparently, banks are also facing a potential existential crisis resulting from technological advances and innovation. The narrative goes something like this:

> Fintechs and non-traditional players will undermine incumbent banks through digital disruption. Big Data, AI and chatbots will drive every banking relationship.

> In this fast-paced, dramatically changing, constantly evolving environment, many trusted and long-lived institutions will fail to adapt, inevitably wither and ultimately die.

> YOU MUST ACT NOW

> Call +800 123 123 for your Big Four consultant

Fear is always an excellent motivator and helps fuel panic that, maybe, your organization isn't doing enough to build towards its future state. In fairness, it's difficult to determine what *enough* really means, since much of the future state remains uncertain, unclear and some years away.

What is certain and clear is that whatever the future looks like, data and analytics will be front and centre of any bank operational model. And unlike many of the elements comprising the future state, you can apply data and analytics today, on today's business problems, and to leverage today's opportunities.

So, investments you make in your data and analytics delivery today will yield immediate *and* longer-term benefits.

There has been tangible progress in using analytics and almost all financial services organisations have invested in building capabilities. But there are often disconnects between the investment and the return; and I still hear comments like "I can't even consider advanced analytics until I can get accurate daily sales data".

Complacency is the greatest danger, maybe believing that enough has been done for now and that current analytical capabilities are *good enough*. Such thinking might prove devastating. Conversely, simply investing to build capabilities is not enough—"build it and they will come" just doesn't work. They need to be the right capabilities, focused on the right opportunities, and integrated into the business in the right way.

The critical question must surely be:
How do you ensure your organisation is a net winner and not a loser?

Whether you want to build an analytics team from scratch, extract more value from the resources you already have, or you want to prepare for an expected onslaught from fintechs, this book will show you how to exploit analytics successfully—identifying the capabilities, the opportunities, and the business integration model.

My purpose here is to demystify and explain analytics, to ensure you are sufficiently well-informed to make smarter decisions about how to build, leverage and profitably deploy your analytical resources.

Upfront, it's important to stress that the focus will be on the exploitation of analytics to deliver meaningful business returns. This pragmatism means real case studies and examples of things that work (and some that don't)—albeit with changes to protect confidentiality.

So, without further ado, let's begin…. we've got a lot of ground to cover.

PART 1

CONTEXT

CHAPTER 1
Introduction and Scope

Over my career, I've built analytical capabilities multiple times—for different organisations, in different geographies and with different states of organisational readiness. Much of what I've learnt (sometimes painfully) is covered in the coming chapters.

A key learning is that, when trying to build capabilities, you need significant engagement with your business partners. Their thinking will probably fall into one of three broad camps:

- Everyone agrees on the need for massive organisational engagement to embrace analytics. This is a start-up mentality, and I've only once experienced this level of determination and focus... after all, it's counter-cultural for most traditional banks.

- Some appreciation of the need for new thinking and using analytics to improve performance, likely in response to declines in margins, ROI, market share or organisational effectiveness. But even though there is support for analytics, understanding and commitment is of varying degrees—not everyone will be on board, even in the face of early successes. Throughout my career, this is a typical situation.

- Extreme resistance to any change in the status quo; any tilt towards data-driven approaches is met with obstacles. This is extreme legacy thinking, often driven by (a) a lack of understanding of "the new", both in approach and impact; and (b) faith and safety in "the old" to deliver the required business goals. Remarkably, such organisations still exist.

An organisation must *at least* recognise that they need to do things differently and are prepared to try—and the more senior the recognition, the more likely analytics will gain traction.

The Key to Building Analytics Capabilities

But it's not just about recognition. Here's my view of the critical elements when building out analytics capabilities. At the risk of extreme simplification and in priority order, they are:

1. ***Organisational readiness.*** Like any business transformation, you need senior support, not just with words but also with actions. There needs to be a commitment to growing analyst resources, instigating test programs and rolling out successes more widely.

   Maybe there's also recognition of a common threat to the status quo—a threat requiring new thinking, new ideas, and/or new approaches.

2. ***Engage, engage, engage.*** Business partners are the most important constituent to the process. This must be a partnership; analytics will fail without their active engagement and help.

   Inevitably, the analytics remit will expand. The organisation will become more familiar and comfortable with the analytics contribution. Additional areas of operation will become more analytically driven. But initially, business partners will be most concerned about potential impacts to the business-as-usual operations. Don't put business goals at risk; ensure complete transparency about what is happening and what to expect; include contingency plans and roll-back options.

   Analytics also needs extensive support and interaction with many other business functions—most critically Finance, Risk Management and Technology. Again, ensure there's deep engagement.

3. ***Don't run before you can walk***. Identify specific use-cases, examples to test highly defined analytical opportunities. Maybe you first prove the value for one product, or segment, or channel, or even a single branch. Once results are proven, expand coverage further.

You should plan for a staged development and ensure that each stage depends on successful outcomes from the previous stages. Be flexible and adjust plans as required.

Developing capabilities can be a frustratingly slow process, and you will need patience. At each step, the organisation must learn and adapt. It will probably take *at least* three-years to embed the right capabilities correctly, even when building out an existing team.

4. ***Measurement is critical.*** Upfront, there must be agreement with business partners about the precise definition of success. Use hard, unequivocal metrics—avoid any doubt in interpreting results. This requirement should inform your decisions on use-cases prioritisation.

5. ***Data and tech are not as important as engagement.*** Issues always exist with data availability and technology readiness. Don't get bogged down in fixing the issues. Prioritise those with the greatest likely business or customer impact and get back to the business engagement because that's where you'll find the value-add.

These are the bare bones you need to consider. Inevitably, the devil is in the detail... and we will get to that.

What We'll Be Covering

This isn't a book about organisational transformation, but I will cover some transformation issues and how to deal with the inevitable transition of turf as analytics capabilities build-out.

What else will we be exploring that can help?

Part 1 is essential reading for senior executives. Banking is dramatically changing, and building analytics capabilities is increasingly critical to defensive and offensive competitive strategies. What needs to be done? What should your analytics roadmap look like?

The remainder of Part 1 offers high-level solutions to these concerns, fleshes out the analytics remit, and sets the scene. Central to this mission is the need to identify *and quantify* the analytical contribution to the business.

Three further sections follow. Part II serves as a primer and covers concepts such as what we mean by big data and how it has evolved. We also look at different types of analytics and some techniques to apply. This is not intended to be an exhaustive technical treatment but provides a grounding for those interested in the techniques or who want to understand what we mean by terms such as "machine learning" and "artificial intelligence".

Part III considers potential application areas and is aimed at senior business managers. Where to start with so many possible applications? We'll cover guidelines on picking winners.

Detailed discussions include analytical opportunities across the customer lifecycle and the importance of listening to customers—observing their interactions, transactions and behaviours, and then responding in an analytical and meaningful way. We also examine key aspects of lead generation and customer relationship management.

Part IV concentrates on execution issues and we'll discuss meaty operational issues here. This should be of acute interest and relevance to analytics leaders and managers. Others might want to cherry-pick their way through.

Implicit in successfully building capabilities is the need for significant business knowledge and interpersonal skills within the analytics group, and particularly from the group leader—this can be a challenge for recruitment and retention. This will be discussed.

We also need to consider other operational issues. How to structure the analytics function, and with what skills? What should be the reporting line? Should you outsource? How to manage data governance and controls (including information security and data privacy)?

As a counterpoint to these serious execution issues, a chapter of bloopers follows—there've been a few of these over the years.

And finally, we'll consider the potential impact on banking and analytics of Covid-19; the "elephant in the room" for everyone's strategy development right now.

Exclusions to Our Discussion

Of necessity, some areas are out of scope:

- **Data availability and storage**. We will talk about data and storage, but we can't get into the detail of what data is potentially available (internal and external) and how it might be pre-processed, manipulated, and physically stored. That said, data specific usage examples are important and will be highlighted, e.g. timeliness of data availability and the impacts on targeting effectiveness.

- **Technology** is an important source of competitive advantage and a business enabler. There's a lot going on, of which here are a few trends.

  The Cloud is forcing radical changes in operating architecture; delivering a storage, processing and service platform that is scalable, secure, robust, and resilient. Distributed ledger technology (DLT, of which blockchain is the most well-known example) is a game-changer, with obvious opportunities in customer identification/KYC and fund-flow audit trails to support AML; other opportunities are emerging.

  The impacts of AI and robotics cannot be understated. Applications include process automation, fraud detection, risk assessment and voice interfaces (including chatbots and virtual assistants).

- **Analytical tools** have proliferated over the last ten years. We now have open-source tools and data/application domain-specific applications. But the need for focus precludes discussion about SAS, SPSS, R, Python, Hadoop, Spark or any other analytical tools, languages, and platforms.

These exclusions are all *analytical enablers* and of themselves, they do not deliver the business transformational analytics we should be seeking. They are important but must remain secondary to our relentless focus on finding how to deliver analytical value.

So, where do we find that value?

Expected Benefits

There's a risk that we might be getting ahead of ourselves, but I think it's important that we "nail our colours to the mast" early on.

Figure 1.1 shows four key areas of benefit from analytics. This is based on my personal view and reflects the types of banks I've worked with. For me, improvements in marketing effectiveness have exceeded 50% on at least two occasions... at well-established banks, with mature marketing functions. These are all achievable and viable deliverables.

Of course, there are a lot of dependencies—not least, your operating model, start-point, mix of products, business activities and resource levels.

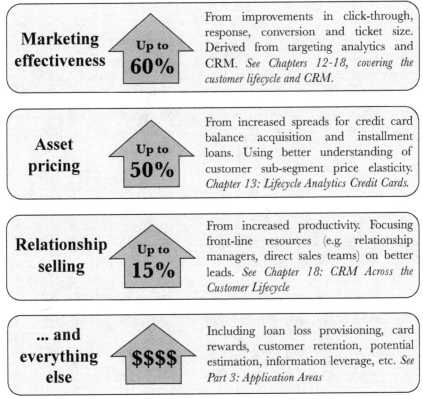

Marketing effectiveness — Up to **60%** — From improvements in click-through, response, conversion and ticket size. Derived from targeting analytics and CRM. *See Chapters 12-18, covering the customer lifecycle and CRM.*

Asset pricing — Up to **50%** — From increased spreads for credit card balance acquisition and installment loans. Using better understanding of customer sub-segment price elasticity. *Chapter 13: Lifecycle Analytics Credit Cards.*

Relationship selling — Up to **15%** — From increased productivity. Focusing front-line resources (e.g. relationship managers, direct sales teams) on better leads. *See Chapter 18: CRM Across the Customer Lifecycle*

... and everything else — **$$$$** — Including loan loss provisioning, card rewards, customer retention, potential estimation, information leverage, etc. *See Part 3: Application Areas*

Figure 1.1 Sources of Benefit from Analytics

So, how do we unlock this value? Let's talk about the analytics remit... the turf it should cover.

CHAPTER 2

Turf'n'Surf

You should already have some form of analytics function within your organisation. Ask yourself a couple of questions about current operations:

- Does everyone (particularly senior management) clearly understand what (and how) analytics contributes to business success?

    Functions like compliance, finance, risk, and marketing all have a clear remit; everyone knows their roles and responsibilities. The situation may be less clear for analytics. It might be operating on the margins, sometimes intersecting and supporting other business functions. This needs to change; the analytics turf needs to be defined.

- Is the contribution from analytics appropriately measured (revenue, profit, or something else) and known?

    Other functions have performance measures that are direct business drivers, and so should analytics. Metrics like "number of completed projects" and "potential business improvement" aren't sufficient. You need hard metrics about real business contributions; and they should be unambiguous, agreed by all, and then published and tracked.

These might appear to be simple questions, but in reality, they are complex, nuanced and indicative of the *place* and *value* of analytics within the organisation.

If you can answer both questions positively, then you are already in a better place than most. For everyone else (probably a large majority), you have a problem, and it's a fundamental problem that strikes to the heart of the organisation's analytics ambition.

It goes back to my assertion that analytics must own meaningful turf. I don't mean something vague like "owning all high-end analytical projects". After all, what do we define as a high-end project? Who decides what to work on? How are the results deployed? Is the contribution measured and meaningful? These decisions involve subjectivity—and human bias, whimsy and emotion. It's not data- or customer-driven.

Analytics Needs to Own Substantive and Meaningful Turf

Turf is vital and here are the key reasons:

- *Collaboration is essential, but so is ownership.* Businesses today are highly collaborative. Successes are shared; challenges are overcome through teamwork; analytics success comes from collaborative effort. But there needs to be some element of business performance that is uniquely owned and recognised as the analytics remit... the turf.

- *Data and analytics should drive, not follow*. Without turf, the opportunities for data and analytics to drive business success are more limited. Analytics becomes a useful contributor rather than an independent force for positive change. It is viewed as a utility function, called upon by the business lines, usually when deemed appropriate to contribute in resolving a particular problem.

  In such an environment, it's difficult to see how analytics can stand out amongst the numerous other competing demands for attention, budget and resources. Transformational change is likely impossible.

- *Delivery of a continuous and significant benefit stream.* Analytics can provide a contribution to almost every aspect of banking, even down to how often to change the lightbulbs in the branches.

  But if you are going to leverage analytics as a competitive advantage, you should not be concentrating on lightbulbs... or any other ad hoc, sporadic or transient opportunities. You need a clearly defined and predictable benefit stream; sufficient to justify the investments needed in analytics resources and capabilities.

The analytics contribution needs to be meaningful (it matters to the business), and significant (it generates a non-trivial business impact). We should not be fiddling around on the margins; we should focus on things that matter.

- ***Do not build a solution searching for a problem.*** Beware the dangers of building analytics capabilities without turf. Any benefits you might expect from investments in big-data and advanced analytical insights will be almost impossible to deliver. I've seen this frequently, where sophisticated analytics functions are fishing for something (anything) to work on, primarily because the business lines don't know how to exploit and engage.

I've also seen voluminous requests for basic reporting rather than real value addition. There's always a pent-up demand for such reports, the stuff informing day-to-day decision making. Whilst I recognise this is important, it is not analytics; it is management information. The analytics function is often the best place to support such MI, but that should not be at the expense of squeezing value-additive activities.

If you want to remain competitive, you must better leverage your customer data... which requires massive use of analytics... together with a recognised continuous, consistent and significant return on analytical effort... and that requires turf. But which turf?

The Core Analytics Turf Components

Analytics core turf must include the remit to answer critical business questions arising from time-to-time. Typical problems might include:

- How do we identify customers with the most untapped opportunity?
- What is driving the deposit volume fall over the last two months?
- What are the product holdings of the most affluent customers?
- Why are mortgage early redemptions rising?
- Why has credit card attrition increased?

This is old-school, well-established analytics turf. Your current analytics sophistication will dictate how easy it is to deliver answers to these kinds of questions. Larger organisations will typically have a dedicated team, smaller banks are often more limited in options. The alarming truth is these kinds of questions (whilst important to the business when they arise) are relatively few and infrequent. Even in a large organisation, you might get 30-50 such queries per year, which equates to just a few dedicated analysts.

Building analytics *at scale* needs different turf, and it needs to be turf delivering continuous, significant and recognised improvements in business performance. Once you get scale, you get fungible resources and the flexibility to apply significant analytical firepower where required.

A key area of the analytics remit should be targeting, including new customer acquisition and existing customer engagement and development.

In reality, targeting comprises multiple components. Activity must be:

- *Targeted* to focus on the most appropriate audience;
- *Tracked* to determine effectiveness;
- *Optimised* to ensure the highest returns;
- *Integrated* with other marketing and sales activities.

Massive analytical contributions can be made in all these areas. If any of these activities are managed outside of the analytics group, then it makes sense to centralise the activity and the expertise.

> **Once analytics has control of the end-to-end targeting, it is not unusual to get like-for-like performance increases of up to 60% over previous approaches**

Let's consider the targeting components in turn.

Traditional Targeting
Whether you're considering engagement on social media or offers delivered via branch sales, targeting increases the relevance and personalisation of messaging and offers.

11

I'm not talking about simply building a customer segmentation or a response prediction model; although that's usually "a good thing". This is so much more.

Best-in-class execution must also incorporate continuous testing of targeting components (audience, offers/messages, channels, pricing, timing)—forever challenging to improve and enhance approaches. This is complex and needs a high level of technical proficiency in design, execution, and performance monitoring.

Offer-in-Context Targeting

Here, we're targeting highly specific behaviours, triggering context aware messages and offers. Customer volumes will be small for each communication (possibly just half a dozen contacts per day) but we might have ten, twenty, one hundred, or more separate behaviours we're looking out for and responding to with different treatments.

Contributors to the context include:

- *Relevance.* These events have high relevance to the customer. There should be a clear association between the observed behaviour and a customer need. If you're making an explicit offer, then the response rate should be high; consider nothing below 10%.

  You can also use predictive modelling to help further refine your behaviour identification and increase response and relevance.

- *Timeliness.* Both the need identified, and the message delivery are potentially time constrained. Communication with the customer will often have urgency and therefore high priority. The longer you leave it, the less relevant the communication, e.g. the opportunity to sell travel insurance disappears once they are on vacation.

- *Location.* Some offers might rely on customer location for either the identification and/or delivery of the offer, e.g. you're in the store, the offer has attractiveness; you leave the store; the offer is far less attractive.

- *Channel.* It's not just which channel the behaviour was identified on; it's also about which is the most appropriate channel to deliver a potential offer (which could easily be different). We'll start the discussion about channel deployment shortly.

The simplest offer might be nothing more than an event-trigger; identifying a behaviour and generating an offer with no other intelligence, e.g. time-deposit maturity triggers a renewal offer. But the most sophisticated can deliver the level of individual recognition and personalisation that customers are increasingly demanding.

Tracking

We're talking here about the management of core campaigns, those that seriously drive the business. They likely represent a significant chunk of budget, but are they adequately tracked? Think about this quote:

> *"I know I'm wasting half my advertising budget.*
> *The problem is... I don't know which half"*
> John Wanamaker (1838—1922)

It's equally applicable to marketing rather than advertising and even today, more than 100 years later, many banks are potentially still wasting a fairly significant proportion of their budget... or at least not adequately tracking, and therefore *not knowing* effectiveness.

Evaluating campaign performance is tricky, it takes skill to design campaigns making measurement possible. But more importantly, it takes commitment to accurate measurement; you've got to want to know the detailed results. And when you're exceeding plan, on budget, and crazy busy, it is easy to let the details slide.

Performance tracking is so important that you should consider *making core campaign performance tracking mandatory*. How do we work out the most appropriate offer if we don't know the historical performance? How can you assess relative channel performance without comparable metrics? How do we optimally allocate sales and marketing resources without the ability to compare across campaigns?

The need for tracking throws up a whole bunch of additional questions about what to measure and how. Chapter 11 starts the discussion about these issues and others related to performance tracking.

Optimisation

Tracking allows us to perform two levels of optimisation:

- Within the campaign, to ensure that the targeting is performing at the optimum and delivering the expected business results. This should be part of a feedback loop to targeting, and particularly the testing regime.

- Across all campaigns, to ensure that the contact opportunity is not wasted. I'm not just talking about the marketing expense of delivering the message; it's also about the window of opportunity you have with the customer. Don't waste that opportunity with the wrong offer.

Optimisation across campaigns needs an integrated approach to campaign and channel management, which requires the use of Customer Relationship Management (CRM) techniques.

Integration

Complexity is inevitably increasing to manage more channels, more personalisation and increased frequency of message delivery. CRM is the mechanism for ensuring that these diverse activities are integrated and coherent (i.e. they make sense and are not contradictory or conflicting when viewed from the recipient's perspective).

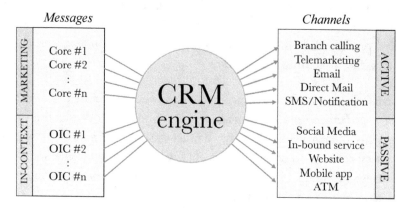

Figure 2.1 CRM Inputs and Outputs

14

CRM provides a framework ensuring all potential communications are assessed and prioritised according to a series of business rules, which might include customer relevance (assumed using estimated response), urgency, channel appropriateness, expected business return, contact history, and prior offer making history. Figure 2.1 shows the approach graphically. We'll consider CRM in more detail in Part III; where complexity "under the hood" is discussed.

This example assumes only core offers and offers-in-context are managed via CRM. A core campaign is significant enough to be executed year-round. Ad hoc marketing communications usually don't need the same level of integration and can be managed using a separate process.

Note that channels can be active or passive. Communications populated to an active channel are always delivered (or at least attempted), whatever the circumstances. But, populating to a passive channel requires waiting for the customer to show up before delivery. If the customer doesn't show up (maybe not logging into the website before the communication validity expired) then there's no delivery.

The most important implication of the passive/active distinction is that you may want to put top priority marketing offers onto active channels only. Of course, passiveness can be at different levels: someone who uses your mobile app every day is far from passive.

Twenty years ago, it was much easier to manage offers and channels. Each channel had a significant delivery cost, and thus less relevant offers would underperform and be discontinued. With the advent of low-cost and high-scale channels (SMS and email initially) "channel abuse" proliferated—millions of customers were targeted with irrelevant offers. Low response and high opt-out rates have been an inevitable consequence. Fortunately, a new generation of marketers are more switched on to the danger of over-contact, the importance of offer relevance, and the perils of abusing customer trust, particularly via social media. But legacy impacts mean that some opt-out rates remain high.

Banks aren't the only perpetrators of channel abuse. Irrelevant and intrusive web display ads from multiple business sectors is often cited by consumers as a driver of the decision to adopt ad blocking software. Initially, blocking was primarily on desktops, now it's increasingly on mobile. The erosion in audience has significantly reduced opportunities for ad placement.

Potential Challenges

The Surf Turf

The use of digital banking platforms and the digitisation of transactions and interactions has exploded in recent years. This has resulted in reduced operational expenses and increased flexibility and convenience to customers—and has forced changes to business and operating models.

But in the rush to digitise, do not forget the customer. With less front-office face-to-face interactions there are fewer opportunities to build relationships. The implications are probably two-fold:

-   Remaining human interactions take on added significance. Complaint handling and human operator supported customer services are becoming the exclusive human face of the organisation for many customers. How to ensure customers remain engaged despite less front-office personnel and fewer customer interactions?

    There needs to be individual customer recognition, and increased personalisation, particularly when offering products or solutions—which should be tailored to an identified need (whether predicted or from an event) and delivered in the most convenient and timely way.

> **Customer Relationship Management**
>   **+ offers-in-context**
>   **+ predictive targeting mechanism**
>
>   **= increased customer engagement**

-   Customers expect their bank to be "joined up". They expect the bank to be coordinated across all channels—in communications and the recognition of customer interactions, transactions and activities.

If a customer has an existing stock trading account, don't offer a new stock trading account when they log onto your website (particularly if the pricing or offers are better than those the customer signed up for).

If a customer is strongly signalling their intention to attrite (we'll talk about some of the signals later), then the top priority on all channels must be to dissuade attrition, maybe with a retention offer.

If an online customer looks at three pages of loans information, finishes on a page detailing interest rates and payment terms, begins (but does not complete) an online application, then calls a customer service hotline... what next? Does your service agent know what just happened? If they do, has an appropriate offer been generated? Is that offer specific to the individual customer or generic to a segment? Maybe the offer is supported by pre-approval criteria or enhanced targeting based upon estimates of customer wealth or income? And is the offer part of a test of customer rate sensitivity (a reasonable hypothesis given the observed behaviour)?

This is an extreme example, and I don't think anyone has these capabilities fully. But it should illustrate what will be possible in the future, and that future-state is not too far away.

> **Customer Relationship Management**
>   **+ offers-in-context**
>   **+ predictive targeting mechanism**
>
>   **= an integrated customer experience**

We have to be joined-up, and we need new thinking to understand what that means. Get the data integrated, get the analytical resources centralised, and treat customers holistically and intelligently.

Business goals

Performance tracking is sometimes inconvenient; it might shine a light on an issue people would prefer was left in the shadows. Like good little worker bees, we've been trained to keep plugging away at a goal even when we know it's a suboptimal use of resources. And the more focussed we become on a goal, the less flexible we can be with those resources, at least until that goal has been achieved.

If analytics is telling us there's a 40% likelihood that a customer will respond to offer A, then why would we make offer B with a 2% response rate? Sometimes, it's because we've hit the goal for offer A and are now totally focussed on plugging the gap for offer B... even though it's dumb and we're failing to address clear customer need. This might be an extreme example, but the underlying behaviour does take place.

The only way out of this trap is to allow a degree of dynamic goal reassignment as circumstances change (subject to certain strategic and business imperatives). That way, the data and the customer are then starting to drive the activities *and the goals*.

Think about how goals are determined, anyway. It's often a finger-in-the-air exercise—albeit reasonably well informed and based on previous years of accumulated knowledge of hits and misses. Goals that are more tightly aligned to customer data and accurate performance expectations will gradually become the norm, but it will take time as we work through the kinks.

Territoriality

Territoriality compounds the problems observed with single-minded goal pursuit.

Any significant business group has a natural tendency to be protective of their customer base. This territoriality can be driven by a genuine desire to protect and nurture customer relationships, e.g. insulating high net worth customers from cold calls. But whatever the reasons, territoriality is counter to the optimisation of contact opportunities and the delivery of the most appropriate offers to customers.

Implementing a CRM approach will markedly reduce (or even eliminate) territorial issues. Offers should be optimised across the organisation, whilst being mindful of the importance of addressing customer needs and business priorities—including the protection of high net worth customers.

Finding the Sweet Spot

The conversation about whom to target, with what, and how, has multiple constituents. So many voices, all with a stake in the game: product owners, marketing, risk management, finance, sales, telemarketing, digital teams and so on. At the risk of sounding trite, the most important voice must be the customer. If there is a clearly signalled need, we must try to satisfy it.

In a more practical and operational sense, we have an optimisation problem; with multiple (potentially competing) objectives from stakeholders and multiple constraints (including channel capacity, budget, contact history, and target volumes).

Channel capacity. There's a fixed element (e.g. permanent sales force, committed media spend, etc), at least in the near term. Variable capacity drawn upon as required (subject to budget constraints).

Business goals. Typically, these are hard metrics e.g. number of new accounts, volume of new sales, proportion of cross-sold accounts, etc.

Optimal targeting. Optimisation is both within different campaigns, and across all activities.

Figure 2.2 The Targeting Sweet Spot

It won't be a seamless process, there will be compromises and horse-trading as you progress towards the sweet spot. It is also an intensely collaborative exercise; everyone must share the same understanding of what you are trying to do and how you will get there.

And in reality, the sweet spot is always moving. But just getting close dramatically improves business performance.

The different elements of the analytics remit are considered in detail in later chapters.

CHAPTER 3

A Brave New World

Undoubtedly, we are living in a period of dramatic changes in how we bank. Technology advances are driving significant innovation in financial products, access, and delivery. Three broad themes are fuelling this innovation:

- Fintechs exploit technology to reimagine how we bank, coming up with new services and radical reworkings of the old. They are agile and unrestricted by legacy systems and legacy customers.

- Techfins are technology companies seeking to flex their scale muscles to introduce financial services leveraging huge customer bases. Alibaba (with Alipay and 1 billion users) blazes the brightest trail, but Apple, Google and Amazon are also amongst those representing a clear and present danger to traditional banks—that that's just in payments.

- Customer expectations are evolving. Increasingly, they want mobile, they want seamless interactions, and they want real-time. They don't want wet signatures, forced branch visits, and multiple days to complete a transaction.

How do these themes impact your strategy for data and analytics?

The Changing Competitive Landscape

The emerging competitive environment between the traditional players and the young upstarts is primarily defined by *legacy*.

Incumbents' enjoy some positive legacy compared with new entrants:

- The strength of the brand and franchise
- High levels of consumer confidence and trust
- Rich understanding of the markets in which they operate
- Deep knowledge of their broad customer bases
- Established policies and operational frameworks

These represent considerable competitive advantage. New players can buy talent and expertise, but other elements of this legacy are far harder to replicate or compete against.

Of course, it's not all plain sailing for the traditional banks. Legacy also has some disadvantages:

- Relatively inflexible and dated operational and transactional platforms
- Large customer bases mean slight changes have far-reaching implications, particularly in pricing and servicing
- It's difficult to lose the traditional mindset and embrace disruptive innovation

And these incumbent disadvantages are precisely the new entrant strengths. They're not encumbered by legacy platforms; they don't have large legacy customer bases to worry about; their business proposition embraces disruptive innovation.

Traditional players must beware complacency. They may have an edge for now, but this is not a stable and balanced yin-yang situation. New entrants will build brand strength, consumer confidence, and contextual understanding… and whilst this will take time, the clock is already ticking.

In tandem, traditional banks are seeking to become more innovative and agile, attempting to shrug off their negative legacy whilst embracing the positive. That must include enhancing analytics to:

(a) better exploit the potential in existing customer bases; and,

(b) improve the identification and fulfilment of customer need.

That's obviously a winning strategy whatever the competitive pressures, and we will discuss plenty of analytical examples and applications in forthcoming chapters.

What other responses might traditional banks mount in the face of new competition? How can analytics support and help?

Fintechs will continue to innovate, and you might eventually (and selectively) either try to acquire (gain a controlling interest) or partner with them. Whatever the approach, they'll need access to partial customer data and maybe some operations and processing. Your level of preparedness for this and the ease of interoperability between you and potential partner systems may give you a crucial competitive advantage versus your peers— even if you're not the biggest player, your flexibility and speed to market might prove critical.

It's a similar situation with techfins. The obvious opportunities are where their own customer base can provide offer-in-context opportunities for new bank relationships, or for expanding an existing customer relationship (for customers of both your bank and your techfin partner).

Other potential partners are out there, capable of providing further opportunities for offers-in-context. Retail chains and telcos look particularly attractive because they are data-rich and have large customer bases.

We need to look at offers-in-context, interoperability and the broader challenges ahead in more detail.

Offers-in-Context

The opportunity is much more than a simple third-party distribution play. We are trying to address consumer need as identified by their interactions with the partner organisation. We aren't simply dumping offers out there in the hope there might be a response. Can you imagine how your third-party partner might feel if that was how you treated their hard-won customers?

As with offers-in-context made to your own banking base, the context here is also driven by relevance, timeliness, location awareness and channel intelligence—but leveraging much of that context from the relationship the customer has with the third party.

The relevance might be signalled exclusively by customer behaviours, or through further enhancement from predictive analytics. Analytics is easier to apply if the target individual is a customer of both the third-party and the bank (there's more observable data and consequently more available insights). For a non-bank customer, we might be able to access external data to enhance our view (data exchanges, social media, credit bureaux), or maybe the third-party relationship data and history (probably unlikely), or possibly core demographics are available via the third-party (more realistic, but still a little skinny).

Elements of CRM should also be considered:

- Offers we make should probably understand the history of offers made to that individual. If the same offer was made last week, is it still relevant? If they refused last week's offer, should we adjust the terms of the current offer?

  The management of offers should incorporate processes for recording the offers made and subsequent response. We should have continuous learning to improve effectiveness and relevance.

- The offer delivery mechanics should be seamless and viewed by the recipient as a natural extension of their interaction. We should not impact the customer experience negatively.

Some opportunities are obvious. When making a large payment, there may be an opportunity for an instant credit facility. Booking overseas travel may signal a need for travel insurance.

Other opportunities are less well signposted. As an organisation, you will need to get creative. Given an observed behaviour, what are the most likely needs of a customer? Develop a hypothesis, test within a small sub-population, measure results and evaluate. If it didn't work, move on to testing the next hypothesis. When you find one that works, scale up.

Interoperability as a Competitive Advantage

Under the probable future operating model, the hunt for fintech and techfin partners will become intense. So why would a strong potential partner choose you? What makes a partnership successful?

The key to success may well be *interoperability*: the ease with which you and a partner successfully collaborate. Interoperability isn't just about systems and technology, it also includes processes, data, cultural fit, goal alignment, people and so much more.

Once you've assigned end-to-end core campaign management and CRM to analytics, it becomes a key component of interoperability. Analytics can ensure:

- Customers are targeted with the best available offers. Any definition of "best available" should include customer need, business return and strategic considerations (like new product launches).

- Predictive analytics are applied as the business norm, and CRM is used to co-ordinate offer delivery. Every effort is made to minimise intrusiveness and maximise relevance.

In such a CRM-driven environment, it should be straightforward to plug-in offers from third parties, and they will automatically find their place within the offer hierarchy. If that isn't immediately clear, then it should be later on when we've had the chance to further explore targeting and CRM.

From a technology perspective, application programming interfaces (APIs) are a key enabler of interoperability. You can develop and deploy APIs allowing third parties to interact with your internal systems and customer data in a highly controlled and pre-defined way.

API development will become a critical business activity, with many opportunities for analytics engagement in that development process. Obviously, any offer-in-context needs to be integrated with other customer CRM driven activities, but there is also a more general consideration of the analytics contribution. It is important to remember technology teams have a deep understanding of data held on your operational systems, but

24

often have a more limited understanding of how the business interprets and uses that data. Typically, interpretive expertise resides in the analytics community. They probably need to be involved in specifying API data exchange components.

The Opportunities Ahead

Maybe you don't buy into the threat posed by fintech and techfin; or maybe you have a different view of required responses from incumbents.

Whatever your perspective, there is one undeniable truth: customer expectations are changing. If you do not deliver real time, mobile, seamless, relevant and context-aware offers, messages, and services, then your business will suffer.

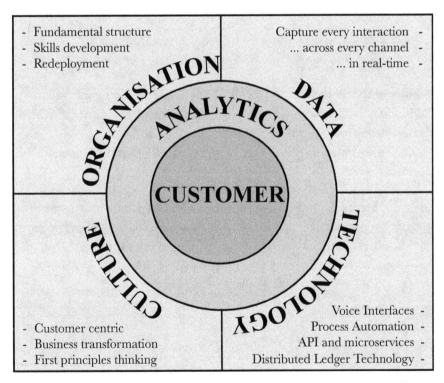

Figure 3.1 Future Opportunities for Banks

Figure 3.1 summarises many of the likely future opportunities. Let's touch on the issues in each quadrant.

Data requirements are changing. A monthly refresh of our databases and a monthly set of broad marketing activities used to be enough. Customers are expecting more. That means upgrading our data infrastructure to widen coverage and incorporate capabilities for real-time capture, recognition and reaction (transactions and interactions driving offer generation).

There are other technology trends. The Cloud is with us today, DLT, Artificial Intelligence and robotics are fast emerging.

Organisational culture will evolve. Customer centricity will become a primary mantra. But evolution is more than simply improving how you do business. It requires *transformation*, and those that are most successful in transforming and evolving will use first principles thinking. For example, don't take the off-line loan application/approval process and just digitise it. Break it down, ask questions (Why is a wet signature needed? Why ask for occupation and income?) and then rebuild it as a better process.

Organisations will change. AI will inevitably displace jobs; people will need to develop new skills and seek redeployment. Analytics is one obvious area of growth, but what else might change? We tend to be organised around products and functions, but what about organising around channels or customer needs?

Finally, in Figure 3.1 the customer is where they should be—at the centre. Analytics represents an enclosing layer, generating valuable business insights, observing behaviours and responding in relevant, intelligent and meaningful ways. It's time to move on and explore what that really means.

PART II

CONCEPTS AND TOOLS

"Big data is like teenage sex: everyone talks about it, nobody really knows how to do it, everyone thinks everyone else is doing it, so everyone claims they are doing it"
Dan Ariely, author and founding member of
the Centre for Advanced Hindsight

"If you torture the data long enough, it will confess"
Ronald Coase, Economist and Nobel Prize Winner (Dec 1910—Sep 2013)

CHAPTER 4

Big Data and How We Got to Now

The thing about big data is that, well... it's *really* big. But any definition simply defining it in terms of bigness is missing the point. The scale implies a need for special treatment, and common definitions say things like "too big to be handled by traditional techniques"—whether those techniques are for physical storage, search/query, analysis or something else.

There is no precise definition of what is "big", as opposed to, say, "very large". Even if there was, it would change as traditional platforms evolve. But (in 2020 terms) big *might* be a petabyte or more for a single dataset.

Before we get too involved with size and scale, we need to take a quick aside to get perspective. You're probably familiar with kilobytes, megabytes, gigabytes and terabytes.

Name	Abbr	Size	Example multiplier
Kilobyte	kB	10^3	1 000
Megabyte	MB	10^6	1 000 000
Gigabyte	GB	10^9	1 000 000 000
Terabyte	TB	10^{12}	1 000 000 000 000
Petabyte	PB	10^{15}	1 000 000 000 000 000
Exabyte	EB	10^{18}	1 000 000 000 000 000 000
Zettabyte	ZB	10^{21}	1 000 000 000 000 000 000 000
Yottabyte	YB	10^{24}	1 000 000 000 000 000 000 000 000

Figure 4.1 International System of Units (SI) Data Sizes

All the formal data sizes are shown in Figure 4.1. As we go down the list, we increase the size 1,000 times at each step. So, a petabyte is 1,000 times larger than a terabyte (or 1,000 terabytes = 1 petabyte). There isn't an officially recognized name for anything larger than a yottabyte, but it may turn out to be brontobyte (10^{27}).

For context, from the dawn of civilization until 1900, the total data ever stored (primarily in books and manuscripts) probably totalled less than 20TB. At the start of the twentieth century, the mechanisms for recording sound and images (both static and moving) were becoming widely available. Our ability to store these different media fuelled a new explosion in data growth. By the end of the last century, all those photos, cassettes, films, CDs, DVDs and the like had probably taken us to maybe 3 or 4 exabytes of total data... ever generated!

We're now generating more than that amount each single day.

A lot of volume growth is fuelled by innovations that are now familiar:

- YouTube (founded in 2004); uploads more than a quarter billion hours of video per day (as of mid-2020). The way we consume entertainment has radically changed.

- Facebook (founded 2005); has 2.7BN active monthly users; uploading 350 million photos and 730 million comments each day. WhatsApp also generates over 100BN messages per day.

- iPhone (launched 2007); over 2BN units sold. Apple didn't invent the mobile phone, but they changed the way we use it. Mobile phones are now both massive consumers and massive generators of data.

A key element of the next significant growth phase will be the Internet of Things and embedded sensors. Projections suggest there could soon be between 30BN and 50BN smart connected devices, each potentially generating a stream of real-time data.

In tandem with our ability to generate data, there has been innovation in storage technology—it's difficult to do one without the other. Hard disks now have an individual capacity up to 20TB and the most advanced solid-state drives (SSDs) can hold 100TB. Artificial DNA storage is one future-tech option, potentially storing a yottabyte in less than a cubic meter; commercially viable products are still a few years away.

So, we generate and store huge amounts of data, but the vast majority of it just sits there... unused, unappreciated and unvalued.

Structured versus Unstructured Data

In reality, big data comprises both structured data and unstructured data. Estimates suggest structured data represents less than 15% of total data.

STRUCTURED DATA	UNSTRUCTURED DATA
Highly organised - There is a data model - There is a data dictionary	Loose data organisation - No data model - Not organized in a defined way
Held in a formal database environment	Significant irregularities, anomalies and ambiguities
Significant standardization (of definitions, formats etc)	Often heavily text based, but can also include voice, images etc
Some level of audit/checking of quality and completeness	Usually unchecked for quality and completeness

Figure 4.2 Structured versus Unstructured Data

Inevitably, the major growth is in unstructured data. Limited effort is needed to load and curate such data. It can be (and often is) just dumped into a *data lake*, presumably under the assumption it will be dealt with (at least analysed and assessed for usefulness) in the future. Yet unstructured data can be powerful, offering supplementary, complementary and contextual understanding to structured data.

For data analytics and many other business applications, unstructured data is a challenge. The attributes of unstructured data are the antithesis of what analysts usually want and need.

For banks, most data we use is structured, and it's likely to remain that way for the foreseeable future. That doesn't mean unstructured data is not available and important. Consider powerful sources of unstructured data that should exist within a bank today.

- ***Web server logs and navigation clickstreams***
  Much of this data has a relatively short-term usefulness (which is just as well given the potential volumes). It is vital for basic website analytics (visits, navigation, etc) and can be leveraged to improve the sales conversion rate.

- ***Channel usage***
  This might not exist, even at a rudimentary level. Customer branch visits? Customer calls to contact centres? Internet/mobile app usage? More useful data would have an indication of the purpose of the interaction. We can infer some of this from transaction logs (e.g. customer made an online payment to a utility company; obviously this assumes there is a channel flag on that transaction data), but it is an incomplete view.

- ***Outbound communications history***
  Every time you communicate with a customer, whatever the media or mechanism, there should be a historical record. This can be a sprawling mass of different files filled with lists of customer numbers and is rarely well organised. Organisation is necessary if you want to employ science in your customer contacts... which you must inevitably do.

To extract continuous value from unstructured data, simple capture and storage is insufficient—and potential future value does not help much in establishing the value of analytics today.

You need to consider where/when/how unstructured data will be used analytically, then introduce a degree of structure to a subset. You will rarely have the time and computing resources to traverse the entire unstructured dataset every time you need to answer a query. When determining the subset composition, consider the most recent stuff and things you use most often. Whilst certain inclusions are obvious (e.g. last login or last time viewed an offer), much will reflect your activities and maturity, and this will evolve. Data mine the unstructured data to find things that have meaning and matter to the business or customer and deliver value.

Social media offers an external source of unstructured data that can improve intelligence on customer preferences and behaviours, market sentiment and advertising effectiveness. Interesting work is also being done using network patterns/composition for (amongst other things) detecting fraud rings and making credit decisions (where bureau is not available). Justification for storing and investing in social media data should be made for specific and clearly defined applications—and performance fully evaluated.

Data Warehousing: A Single Source of Truth

More work is required by most everyone on their use of unstructured data. Much of it will need data point-of-capture redesign or introducing new mechanisms for such capture.

The acquisition and handling of structured data is far more mature, and storage techniques and access methods are well understood... usually using data warehousing. A warehouse represents a single repository of all the information necessary to support reporting, analysis and lead generation; derived from multiple upstream operational systems and looking back through time. Whilst it is often referred to as "a single source of truth", the reality is more nuanced; done well and used appropriately, warehousing *can and should* represent a single source of truth.

With such a consolidated approach, we can use the warehouse as the single source for subsequent (downstream) reporting; for finance, marketing, business heads, and others. This confers multiple advantages:

- There's a significant reduction of inconsistencies between reports since all reports use the same base data.

- It provides a consolidated view of the customer (if designed well); core demographics, product holdings, transactions, etc.

- There may be limits on the historical data held by operational systems. No such constraints exist with a warehouse (unless they are self-imposed).

- The processes for loading data updates (referred to as extract, transform and load, or ETL) provide opportunities for (a) patching glitches; (b) standardising inconsistencies between systems; (c) aggregations, combinations and transformations to generate new variables; and (d) any other background tweaks to the data as necessary.

  Do these things once, when the data loads, rather than multiple times every time the data is used.

You need a single source of truth, and it needs to be resilient, robust, and as complete as possible. It also needs to be managed actively by the analytics function, and that takes dedicated resources and expertise in data management.

Future Considerations

Customers are increasingly carrying out traditional banking activities across multiple platforms and even vendors. Virtual wallets and payment gateways are examples. Your data environment should reflect this.

It used to be that interactions with customers were fairly simple; most activity was driven by the call centre, branch or ATM. Understanding customer channel preferences was not a big deal. Monitoring the impact of different media on marketing offers was also less important. Things have changed, and your data environment needs to reflect this. That environment must continuously evolve, and it needs to include unstructured data.

An even greater challenge is the need for real time data changes and offer deployment. You don't have to update your entire warehouse in real-time; but you will need a mechanism to identify key data changes, e.g. customer has logged in to mobile app, customer has performed a certain transaction, customer has browsed loan interest rate information pages.

Remember, data is the lifeblood of your analytics, and analytics is an increasingly important competitive advantage.

CHAPTER 5

Data Analytics Essentials

The Analytical Spectrum

Analytics has different levels of complexity. As complexity increases, you should see higher levels of business benefit (assuming that you're doing things right).

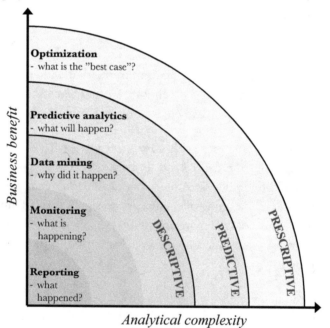

Figure 5.1 Analytical Spectrum

Figure 5.1 shows a representation of complexity versus business benefit over the spectrum of analytical activities. I think it was SAS that first came out with this type of visualisation. Many have used it in various forms since; this is my take on it.

The lowest three tiers represent descriptive analytics: trying to describe situations or circumstances that occurred in the past (which could be very recent).

Data mining is the most sophisticated of the descriptive approaches—often trying to determine *why* something occurred, through the exploration and investigation of historical data, and requiring significant subject-matter and problem domain expertise.

Predictive analytics is forward looking, attempting to predict the future using data from the past. Will a customer buy our product? Will they pay us back on time? Does the company have sufficient liquidity to absorb bad debts? What will interest margins be in the next six months?

The final layer covers optimisation: identifying the best approach from a variety of scenarios. What price should we charge? Which marketing offer should we make? Since the output of optimisation is telling us what we should do, we term this layer prescriptive analytics.

Together, data mining, predictive analytics and optimisation represent advanced analytics.

Across the Universe

I am a strong advocate of the analytics organisation operating across the entire spectrum. You shouldn't have an analytics function that only does, say, predictive modelling. Why?

First, mastery of any tier requires mastery of the tiers below. Each level of mastery builds experience and understanding of the actual data and the data platform. Simply put, analysts learn what data does what, and what are the best candidates for building different solutions.

Understanding the business context is critical for successful analytics. Context is likely to be richer when your work covers the spectrum—and you can more easily access expertise and output from lower layers. If you're interacting with business units for delivery of different types of analysis, then the engagement is also richer.

Finally, analytics across all the layers needs to be centralised. I'm not talking about *operational* reporting here; that should usually remain in the individual operational areas. But business reporting, together with any other business analytics, should be centralised.

Centralisation is necessary because:

- You need a single source of interpretive truth, whether at an apparently trivial level (e.g. how many new customers did we book yesterday?) or more complex (e.g. what constitutes customer attrition: zero balance, long inactivity or physical account closure?). You can't have conflicting numbers between different information sources.

- You cannot have multiple sources of advanced analytical solutions either. This isn't just to ensure consistent interpretations. High-end analytical talent is relatively scarce and scattering such resources throughout the organisation is hugely inefficient.

- Understanding the complete scope and coverage of business reporting inevitably highlights opportunities for rationalisation and consistency. Maybe we're removing duplication or standardising on a common set of metrics for similar reports. Maybe we're just ensuring every report uses the same definition a week (Sun to Sat, or Mon to Sun).

- Building scale brings execution efficiency. Spikes in demand requiring either vertical subject matter expertise or data domain expertise are more easily managed with scale.

- The spectrum is also a career path for analysts. Introduce juniors to basic work and then advance them through tiers as experience grows.

The only exclusion to centralisation is Risk Management analytics. This requires specific and deep domain expertise, and (more importantly) a separation of responsibilities—there's a reason you don't sign-off on your own expenses. It's justifiable for Risk to focus on advanced analytics, whilst reporting and monitoring are included in centralised delivery. But, to make such an approach work, you need a high level of development maturity within the centralised analytics function.

The biggest challenge when operating across all tiers is to ensure sufficient resources are decked against higher contribution activities. The urgency of "the here and now" is impossible to ignore and difficult to manage. Priority must be given to information requests from regulators, reporting on potential compliance gaps, and recovery from customer service failures. And then you've got the product priorities and three hundred branch staff who need sales leads to call... right now.

Managing across the spectrum requires detailed project tracking and resource planning.

Hard versus Soft Problems

A further complication is the difference between hard and soft problems. Consider the graphic in Figure 5.2.

SOFT	HARD
• **High level of uncertainty**	• *Precisely defined*
• **Vague or unstructured**	• *Unambiguous*
• **Diverse views about the actual definition of the problem**	• *Potential single solution*
	• *Well behaved*

Figure 5.2 Hard vs Soft Problems

All problems occupy a point on a continuum: from soft to hard. Soft problems are tricky and shrouded in uncertainty, even about the nature and definition of the problem. Conversely, hard problems are highly defined, and very clear; there may even be a single solution that is stable and unequivocal.

Soft problems typically mean significant interaction with the business to refine requirements iteratively, trying to find a viable and acceptable intersection between the business need and the analytical possibilities.

As a general rule, the more experienced and business-engaged the analyst, the softer the problems they can undertake. Experience means they may have seen a similar issue previously that might give insights into the analytical issue under consideration. And business engagement delivers contextual understanding.

More generally, analytical solutions to soft problems often require higher levels of recognition, understanding, and appreciation of different contextual elements. This is summarised in figure 5.3 below.

Market context	The competitive situation and market norms, including: - Market growth - Competitive activity (acquisition, balances, etc) - Credit environment
Historical context	What we did to get us to where we are, including: - Goals and actions - New product launches - Branch openings
Business context	Financial, operational and strategic issues, including: - Spreads and margins - Credit and lending criteria - Campaign performance assumptions
Problem context	Data, evaluation and interpretation, including: - Data availability, completeness and accuracy - Population size (for assessment or evaluation) - Performance window

Figure 5.3 Different Aspects of Analytical Context

The Analytical Process

Resolving ambiguity and ensuring a reasonable degree of problem hardness is an important part of the analytical process. Softer problems inevitably carry more business risk—the analytics might not deliver a viable solution, or there might be a need for significant rework later on.

Resolving softness in a proposed project needs senior analytical leadership, working with the business to agree what is truly required and viable. Many projects are sufficiently well resolved from the outset, but viability also needs to consider issues such as appropriate data availability—there might be insufficient product take-up information, or the performance period is too recent.

Consideration then needs to be given to other aspects of project definition, such as business criticality, expected outcome, potential business returns, estimated resource requirements to deliver, and the project timeline.

The typical stages involved developing a customer targeting model are shown in figure 5.4.

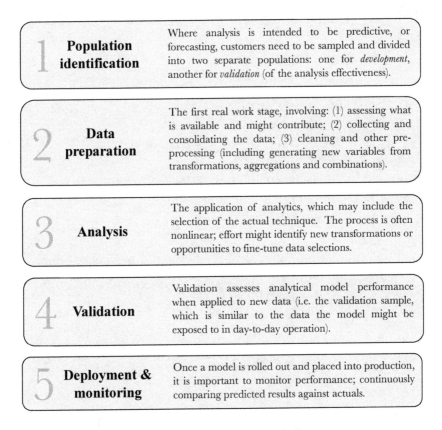

1 Population identification
Where analysis is intended to be predictive, or forecasting, customers need to be sampled and divided into two separate populations: one for *development*, another for *validation* (of the analysis effectiveness).

2 Data preparation
The first real work stage, involving: (1) assessing what is available and might contribute; (2) collecting and consolidating the data; (3) cleaning and other pre-processing (including generating new variables from transformations, aggregations and combinations).

3 Analysis
The application of analytics, which may include the selection of the actual technique. The process is often nonlinear; effort might identify new transformations or opportunities to fine-tune data selections.

4 Validation
Validation assesses analytical model performance when applied to new data (i.e. the validation sample, which is similar to the data the model might be exposed to in day-to-day operation).

5 Deployment & monitoring
Once a model is rolled out and placed into production, it is important to monitor performance; continuously comparing predicted results against actuals.

Figure 5.4 The Targeting Analytic Process

Any analysis ages and becomes less predictive or relevant over time. This makes sense since the external environment is changing, which may also influence customer behaviours.

But we also create changes. We target customer groups using our models. Assuming even modest success, that activity changes the composition of the underlying population (targets respond and therefore are no longer targets).

The faster the changes in the underlying population, the sooner you need to redo the analysis. You can get away with a partial do-over sometimes, which doesn't need a complete redevelopment, only a recalibration of attributes—a considerable saving in time, but a short-term fix only.

Ironically, the more accurate and effective our targeting predictions, the faster we have to remake them.

CHAPTER 6

Descriptive Analytics Toolbox

The last chapter gave you an insight into the analytical process. It's also useful to understand a little about analytical techniques. We will cover this in the next few chapters.

The importance of understanding these techniques depends on you. If you wish, you can skip straight to the discussion of application areas in Part III. Later discussions will reference a small amount of the technical details shown in these toolbox chapters; understanding those details is not essential.

This chapter will consider descriptive analytics, which uses historical information to describe a situation or set of circumstances. In reality, we use vast amounts of descriptive data every day, particularly when summarising business activity for reporting.

Many business situations requiring further investigation use descriptive analytics as the first line of attack. Here are typical examples:

- What's the net change in time deposit volumes year-to-date?

- What are the monthly write-offs for personal loans last 12 months?

- Which customer groups are paying down mortgages early?

- Why is there an uptick in reward redemptions?

Answering these and similar questions is relatively easy, using standard tools and data exploration to build a solution. A further set of descriptive approaches takes things to the next level.

Market Segmentation

Before we get into the toolbox, we need a quick consideration of market segmentation: the act of dividing a population into several distinct, discrete and meaningful segments (or sub-populations).

Distinct: all members of the segment display similar attributes
Discrete: segments are markedly different from each other
Meaningful: you can use them for a purpose, e.g. making an offer

DEMOGRAPHIC	BEHAVIOURAL	FINANCIAL
Affluence	Borrow/Lend	High/Low AUM
Age	F&B/T&E	Revenue
Gender	Risk Profile	Credit/Risk

Figure 6.1 Example Segmentation Schemes

Within banking, segmentation is everywhere. It's primarily used to divide up a large amorphous mass of customers (or prospects) into more manageable sub-groups. It happens in proposition (Premium, Core, Mass), in products (Platinum, Gold, Silver, or co-brands) and in customer treatment (senior/junior/telephone relationship manager).

Segmentation is "old school", and it's over 20 years since one-to-one marketing was making a buzz and advocating the treatment of customers as unique segments of a single customer. Such advocacy was really about driving the understanding of customers as individuals, with specific needs and circumstances.

Customers are now increasingly expecting more personalisation and recognition of their uniqueness—particularly in their transactional and channel behaviours. This is not inconsistent with the use of large segments. The recognition of individual customer transactions and behaviours (and intelligent responses to these) are perfectly viable with appropriate offers-in-context and the application of CRM disciplines—all operating within the broader segment definitions.

Toolbox: Recency, Frequency, Monetary Value (RFM)

Discussion of segmentation leads us, rather nicely, to the first analytical technique in our toolbox: RFM. Typically, the technique is a simple way to segment existing customers, say to identify those who are more/less engaged. It is often used for targeting offers.

Customers are measured across three dimensions and assigned a value, depending upon observed behaviour. The dimensions are:

> *Recency*: How recently did the customer purchase?
> *Frequency*: How often does the customer purchase?
> *Monetary Value*: How much do they spend?

Consider the example in Figure 6.2. Each dimension can take one of three values. So, the range of possible values is 333 (the most engaged customers) to 111 (the least). The specific application will determine what metrics to report for each segment, e.g. average loan size, deposit balances, investment cross-sell ratios, the 12-month attrition rate.

RECENCY	FREQUENCY	MONETARY VALUE
3 = last month	3 = 10 per year	3 = >$500
2 = last 6 months	2 = 5 per year	2 = > $250
1 = longer	1 = less	1 = less

Figure 6.2 RFM Example

In this example, each dimension has three values, but the detailed definitions are flexible. Resist the temptation to jump straight to large numbers of segments from the outset; they should develop gradually as the analytical story unfolds.

If you need a quick way to increase the number of segments used in targeting, then consider RFM. It is simple to develop, explain and deploy.

Note that it can also be used to build a kind of heuristic score, loosely predicting response (say) based upon rankings derived from previous experience.

Toolbox: Clustering

Clustering is another form of segmentation, so each cluster needs to be distinct, discrete and meaningful.

Clustering will group customers with similar characteristics or behaviours, However, clustering also explicitly includes two rules to apply when building the solution:

- Each cluster should maximise the similarities within the cluster;
- Each cluster should maximise the differences with other clusters.

Look at Figure 6.3 below, which displays 20 customers (it's a simplification) according to the value of two attributes A and B.

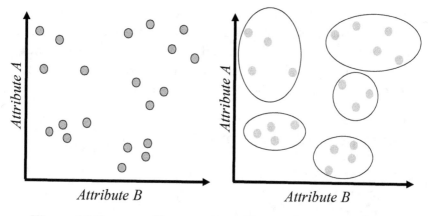

Figure 6.3 Customer Plot   **Figure 6.4** Potential Clustering

Figure 6.4 shows a potential clustering that tries to conform to the two basic rules of similarity and difference.

In the real-world, we'd be using many customers and a variety of different attributes when building a clustering. As usual with all advanced analytics techniques, the variables selected for inclusion can drive the type of solution output, e.g. use credit/risk related variables as attributes, the output is a risk segmentation.

Much of the analytical fun with clustering is trying to visualise the resulting output and translating the individual clusters into language meaningful for the business.

Figure 6.5 shows four segments (of sixteen) from a credit card spending segmentation built for a US card business.

Happy families
- Medium spend
- Low revolve
- Supermarkets dominant
- Pattern suggests kids

Champagne and caviar
- Upscale retailers
- Jewelry and watches
- High average ticket
- High monthly spend

Road Warriors
- High T&E
- Significant out-of-town transactions
- High overseas

Strugglers
- Low ticket sizes
- Convenience stores
- ATM usage
- Low lines

Figure 6.5 Card Spending Segment Examples

Clustering is powerful at taking a lot of variables and classifying customers in an easily understood way, particularly for marketing applications.

But this strength is also a potential weakness. It is not the best way to identify a specific behaviour or response to a marketing offer. Successful applications include:

- Lifestyle segments that can target specific offers and/or rewards appropriate to each sub-group;

- Behavioural segments to provide insights for potential new products;

- Tailoring the language/tone of marketing and sales communications

Clustering remains a niche application of analytics for most; it's pretty complicated and technical.

But it can be astonishingly effective at delivering marketing insights through integrating diverse and unrelated data sources. Geodemographics is the standout example of how successful clustering can be—ACORN and Mosaic are two off-the-shelf solutions available in a variety of markets.

CHAPTER 7

Predictive Analytics Toolbox

Predictive analytics uses historical behaviour to predict future behaviours. We traditionally use two techniques: regression and decision trees. A bunch of further techniques are derived from them.

Toolbox: Regression

Also known as scorecards, particularly within risk management functions, who have historically been heavy users of the technique. Regression uses the characteristics of sample observations to predict an outcome.

Regression has been applied to credit/risk related decisions from the 1950s and began as a manual process. The principles remain the same today: if a customer accumulates sufficient points, they pass an approval threshold.

Let's say existing customers have data on age, occupation, gender and wealth. For new customers, wealth is missing. How can regression help?

Linear regression attempts to predict a continuous output. With our customer data, we could develop a model to predict wealth for any new customer if the age, occupation, and gender are known.

What about trying to predict a single outcome, e.g. wealth more/less than USD1 million? We'd use *logistic regression*, which delivers a probability of the outcome (from 0 meaning no chance to 1 indicating certainty).

Let's have a quick review of regression theory; it's one page only. If you find the maths a little daunting, you can skip the page and go to the practical applications that follow.

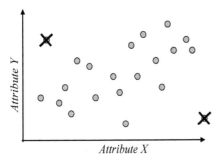

Figure 7.1 Customer Plot

Consider the dataset in Figure 7.1. For each customer, we measure two attributes (X and Y). Each point represents one customer.

First, we remove two outliers (out-of-pattern observations).

The analysis finds the best-fitting line through all the data points. The slope of the line is the gradient (m), derived from the change in y divided by the change in x. The equation for this line is therefore **y = mx + c**

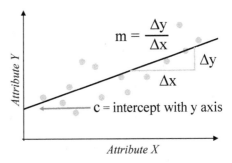

Figure 7.2 Regression Line

This simple linear regression example uses two attributes (x and y); and m defines the weighting to apply to attribute x. For any value of x, we can estimate the value of y. With more variables, the equation gets more complicated, but it's actually straightforward:

$$y = m_1x_1 + m_2x_2 + m_3x_3 + \ldots + m_nx_n + c$$

where: x_n is the nth attribute and m_n is its weight

The levels of fit reflect the strength of the trend in the data. The correlation coefficient (R) measures how good the fit is: 1 = strong positive; 0 = no relationship; -1 = strong negative relationship. Here are some examples:

R = -0.6   **R = 0.0**   **R = +0.6**

47

So much for the theory, what does all this mean in practice?

Take a look at Figure 7.3. This shows the typical (simplified) output from a completed logistic regression scorecard. Variables (representing the attributes) are shown with their associated weights.

Variable description	Weight
INTERCEPT = -3.5178	
# asset products held	-0.3654
# cards held	0.2682
Spend on credit protection last months	0.5336
# dependents	0.1175
Low response occupations like bank officer, director	-0.5492
Low response occupations like snr manager, pilot	-3.2232
High response occupations like technician, clerical	0.6514
Low behaviour score (500 - 602)	0.3070
Utilities transaction in the last two months	-0.2948

Figure 7.3 Scorecard Output

This scorecard is designed to be applied to credit card customers: the higher the calculated score, the more likely the customer will accept a balance transfer offer.

You normally can assume a negative weight means a negative contribution to the score (versus a positive), but don't assume a higher weight means higher importance. Look at the description and the weight together to determine what the directional and scale impact will be on the score.

Here's a couple of things we might infer from the scorecard above:

- The more kids they have, the more likely to accept a balance transfer offer. As a parent that rings true for me.

- The more asset products the customer has, the less likely they are to take a balance transfer. This makes sense in two ways: (1) their lending needs are fully met (the good interpretation); or (2) they are stressed and are unlikely to get approved for further exposure. Two very different interpretations, and if a deeper understanding is important, further investigation is merited.

A popular way to show the impact of a scorecard is through the use of a gains table and gains chart. The tabular results are shown in Figure 7.4.

Decile	#obs	%obs	Cumulative observations	Predicted response rate	Cumulative response rate	Cumulative responses
1	1,407	10.0%	10.0%	8.69%	8.69%	28.24%
2	1,403	10.0%	20.0%	5.05%	6.87%	44.61%
3	1,410	10.0%	30.0%	3.87%	5.87%	57.22%
4	1,320	9.4%	39.4%	3.31%	5.26%	67.31%
5	1,410	10.0%	49.4%	2.59%	4.72%	75.75%
6	1,490	10.6%	60.0%	2.23%	4.28%	83.42%
7	1,407	10.0%	70.0%	1.85%	3.93%	89.43%
8	1,409	10.0%	80.0%	1.56%	3.63%	94.51%
9	1,406	10.0%	90.0%	1.24%	3.37%	98.54%
10	1,405	10.0%	100.0%	0.45%	3.08%	100.00%
Total	14,067	100.0%		3.08%		

Figure 7.4 Gains Table

The total sample is divided into 10 deciles, each representing 10% of the total (or at least as close as possible given the distribution of scores). You could divide by another number, e.g. 20 ventiles or 100 percentiles.

For each decile, the predicted response is the rate for all the customers covered by that decile.

In this example, if we were to target the top 5 deciles:

- We would contact 49.4% of the total population;

- From the cumulative response rate, it predicts us to achieve a 4.72% response rate for the total target group (and 8.69% for decile 1 targets, 5.05% for decile 2 targets and so on);

- The cumulative responses show that we capture 75.75% of the total possible responses. One interpretation is that we saved on contacting 50% of the available targets and only lost 25% of the possible responses.

The predicted cumulative responses can also be shown graphically (Figure 7.5), comparing the results against a random selection from the population.

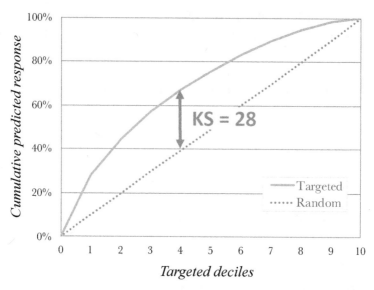

Figure 7.5 Gains Chart

Obviously, random selection delivers the same response rate no matter how many customers we target, hence a straight line.

The point of maximum separation is at decile 4. Separation is measured by the KS score[1]. At decile 4 we are targeting 39.4% of the population, achieving 67.31% of total responses (67.3 - 39.4 = 27.9). All other considerations being equal, this is the most efficient population to target.

The higher the KS, the better. A score below 20 probably indicates the need to adopt a different technique or some other form of reworking.

Final comments on scorecards....

They work well with inputs of continuous data (e.g. number of times past due, age, income, account balance).

There're not so good with categorical data input (e.g. gender, product types, residential city), but they can be rigged to accept it, particularly if there is an inherent hierarchy to the categories (e.g. card type Silver, Gold, Platinum).

---

[1] From Russian mathematicians Andrey Kolmogorov and Nikolai Smirov

Toolbox: Decision Trees

Decision trees are relatively easy to use and produce unambiguous and clear results. The final tree is used to predict an outcome.

Different decision tree techniques all share the same basics:

- The tree starts with a *root node*;

- It grows from the root by branching into *leaf nodes*;

- Leaf nodes can also branch into further leaf nodes;

- The process continues until the tree is determined to be complete (according to a variety of *stopping criteria*).

This is best illustrated using an example, and a technique called CHAID (Chi-squared Automatic Interaction Detection). In this example, we are attempting to improve the response rate of campaigns to sell currency-linked deposits (CLD). Familiarity with the product is not important here. We don't have any campaign data, but we do know which customers have the CLD product. We are therefore building a *look-alike* model.

We have the following variables:

- Premium customer (or not) flag

- Number of deposit products held

- Number of product groups held

- Total footings (all money, across all accounts, in USD)

- Number of multi-currency deposit products

All available variables are considered, and a determination is made about the best variable for "pulling apart" the population (using a technique called Chi-squared testing). New leaf nodes are then formed, and the process continues for each of the new leaf nodes.

Figure 7.6 shows the state of the tree after two iterations. You can see the total population in the root node (we started with 461,874 customers with a take-up rate of 0.30%).

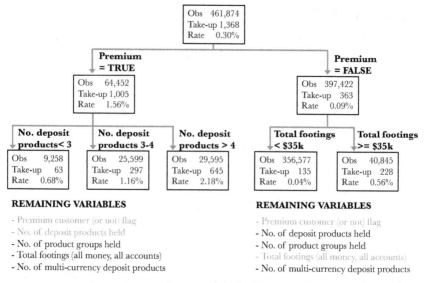

Figure 7.6 Interim CHAID Tree

The first split was made on whether the customer was premium. That improved the take-up rate for premium customers to 1.56% (1,005 take-ups from 64,452 observations). For these customers on the left side of the tree, the next best split was the number of deposit products held. For the right side, the next best split was the total footings. We now have five potential target nodes, with take-up rates between 0.04% and 2.18%.

The first split (premium or not) was a simple true/false and generated two new leaf nodes. The next splits needed to identify how many new leaf nodes were appropriate and which values to use. On the left, there was no statistically significant difference between customers with 0, 1 or 2 deposit products; they are grouped together as <3. It was a similar situation for customers with 3 or 4 deposit products; also grouped. On the right, only one significant split was found, at $35k total footings.

At each stage, the tree only grows using previously unused variables. Each of the three left-most end-nodes has three remaining variables to consider. This is a different set of variables to those under consideration for the two end-nodes on the right.

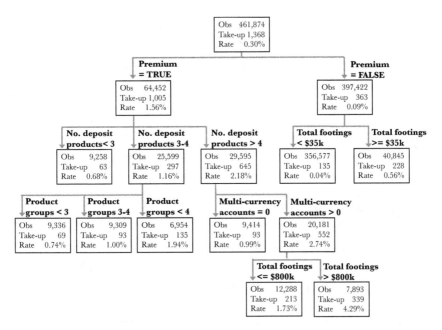

Figure 7.7 Final CHAID Tree

The final tree, shown in Figure 7.7, has nine terminal nodes (those with no further splits) and take-up rates from 0.04% lowest to 4.29% highest. As with regression, we can show results in the form of a Gains table (Figure 7.8) or a Gains chart (not shown).

Node	#obs	%obs	Cumulative observations	Predicted takeup %	Cumulative takeup%	Cumulative takeups
15	7,893	1.7%	1.7%	4.29%	4.29%	24.78%
9	6,954	1.5%	3.2%	1.94%	3.19%	34.65%
14	12,288	2.7%	5.9%	1.73%	2.53%	50.22%
10	9,309	2.0%	7.9%	1.00%	2.14%	57.02%
12	9,414	2.0%	9.9%	0.99%	1.90%	63.82%
11	9,336	2.0%	12.0%	0.74%	1.71%	68.86%
4	9,258	2.0%	14.0%	0.68%	1.56%	73.46%
7	40,845	8.8%	22.8%	0.56%	1.17%	90.13%
8	356,577	77.2%	100.0%	0.04%	0.30%	100.00%
Total	461,874	100.0%		0.30%		

Figure 7.8 Gains Table

The terminal nodes have been rank ordered by the predicted take-up rate. If we concentrate on the top five terminal nodes (15 to 12), we would capture 9.9% of the total base population, and 63.82% of all customers to take up the product.

The look-alike model is clearly effective in identifying the characteristics of customers who have previously taken up the CLD product. The next stage would be to test whether the model was a good proxy for response in a marketing campaign.

Closing thoughts on decision trees...

CHAID works well with categorical data. If you want to use continuous data (like numbers), a tree technique like CART might be more appropriate and can incorporate both classification and regression.

Trees are prone to *over-fitting*; they work well on the data they were given in development, but when applied to the real-world do not display similar levels of performance. As a rough rule of thumb, the deeper the tree, the higher likelihood of over-fitting. Random Forest approaches (building a bunch of different trees and consolidating results) dramatically reduce over-fitting but need significantly more computing power—which may still be an issue for some.

Propensity versus Response Models

Think of propensity models as look-alike, such that:

- Customers who purchased Product X typically have specific and measured characteristics (identified by regression or decision tree results);

- Similar looking customers are assumed to be similarly attracted to Product X;

- As shown earlier, you then have options to decide how tightly you want to target customers with Product X offers. Tighter targeting equals higher response (or at least closer look-alikeness) but smaller volumes.

The benefit of propensity modelling is that identifying the target is painless, and it doesn't involve the collection of new data from the customer.

But it assumes a look-alike really wants the product more than anyone else. Here's an extreme example: if we only ever marketed Product X to females, aged 50+ then guess what a look-alike model will tell us is the best target audience for further Product X sales? Yep, females over 50.

A response model uses response data, which requires making an offer and collecting the results. The process goes like this:

1. Generate a random sample of customers who've never purchased Product X. The sample needs to be large enough to generate enough responses to model robustly. Statistical techniques exist to determine the sample size given the expected response rate.

2. Make all of them an offer (maybe via email, direct mail, telemarketing or some other channel), and collect the responses.

3. Build your model comparing all those who responded, against those who didn't.

Unlike the propensity approach, we've got real data on what customers will do when they see the offer. This is powerful, and the analytical output is highly predictive.

However, response modelling comes at a relatively high cost. First, the response rate is low (because you're turning off all targeting to generate the sample) and you therefore need a large sample. You might use precious sales resources or budgets that could be employed elsewhere to generate revenue more efficiently. Finally, it takes time to gather the data; time you might not have. There are clear trade-offs.

Experience has taught me it is difficult to convince business heads of the incremental benefit from response modelling. They are far more comfortable with propensity modelling.

Interestingly, that comfort is usually not due to budgetary concerns, but because there's a lower impact on business momentum.

Try to use response modelling for your core offers, those that are the biggest drivers of business results. Otherwise, test the use of propensity models—the look-alike approach will often deliver viable performance lifts.

Warning: Correlation Does Not Imply Causality

One more warning before we close out. Just because two variables are seen to move together (and are therefore highly correlated), it does not mean one causes the other... but it might.

For example: Does higher product holdings lead to higher customer retention? The answer is most definitely yes; although there's complexity about why this might be true—it might be that more products is demonstrative of a deeper or more robust relationship, or maybe it's just harder to unwind the relationship with more products.

Here are some more examples where two attributes are highly correlated, and an impact might be inferred.

- Higher deposit balances lead to higher investment balances?
  It's probably true that deposits lead to investments

- Larger shelf space generates higher sales?
  Usually, it's the opposite. Higher sales lead a retailer to allocate more space

- US spending on science, space and tech causes higher suicides by suffocation, strangulation and drowning?
  Pure coincidence, with a correlation coefficient of 99.79%

- Increased ice cream sales leads to increased drownings?
  Nope, it's a third factor driving both... time of year

- Higher CO_2 emissions cause increased obesity?
  Another third factor impact. Increased affluence leads to both higher CO_2 emissions and increased obesity.

CHAPTER 8

The Rise of the Machines

The buzz about Artificial Intelligence (AI) and Machine Learning (ML) seems relentless. Examples of applications in autonomous vehicles, robotics and customer service are ensuring plenty of media interest, scrutiny and reporting.

For some sectors of current economic activity, the impacts will be profound, particularly in displacing human workers and the attendant implications.

But what are the likely impacts on analytics? And what are the possible risks and opportunities?

Let's start with a clarification. Machine learning is just one component of AI, which more broadly also includes language processing and speech, vision systems, robotics, expert systems and so on. From a banking analytics perspective, we should concern ourselves with ML rather than the broader AI landscape.

In simple terms, machine learning is where a computer learns from experience to get better at performing a particular task. We can categorise machine learning into three broad types:

- *Supervised learning* takes specific examples with a known outcome and attempts to build a mechanism to predict future outcomes. This includes our typical analytics for risk scorecards and campaign response prediction.

- *Unsupervised learning* takes examples and attempts to find a structure or pattern in the data. There is no predetermined outcome. An example might include cluster analysis of customers.

- *Reinforcement learning* is more of a trail-and-error approach. Each time a test is made, the algorithm receives a positive or negative feedback as reinforcement. These approaches are used for applications like autonomous vehicles or teaching a computer to play chess.

For problems requiring unsupervised or reinforcement learning, the primary analytical technique is neural networks, so we'll need to add these to our toolbox.

Toolbox: Neural Networks

As the name suggests, neural networks are inspired by biology and are an attempt to produce a simplified model of the brain. An example of how a network might look is shown in Figure 8.1.

Node	#obs	%obs	Cumulative observations	Predicted takeup %	Cumulative takeup%	Cumulative takeups
15	7,893	1.7%	1.7%	4.29%	4.29%	24.78%
9	6,954	1.5%	3.2%	1.94%	3.19%	34.65%
14	12,288	2.7%	5.9%	1.73%	2.53%	50.22%
10	9,309	2.0%	7.9%	1.00%	2.14%	57.02%
12	9,414	2.0%	9.9%	0.99%	1.90%	63.82%
11	9,336	2.0%	12.0%	0.74%	1.71%	68.86%
4	9,258	2.0%	14.0%	0.68%	1.56%	73.46%
7	40,845	8.8%	22.8%	0.56%	1.17%	90.13%
8	356,577	77.2%	100.0%	0.04%	0.30%	100.00%
Total	461,874	100.0%		0.30%		

Figure 8.1 Example Neural Network

Each layer comprises a series of nodes. The input layer represents the data to be presented to the network, and the output layer represents the solution. The intermediate layer(s) between input and output represent the inner workings of the network and are called *hidden*.

Think of the input nodes as different variables: age, sex, gender, income, product holdings. Conceptually, you could have many thousands of input nodes but, in reality, for our applications it's considerably less. You might start out with a few hundred and gradually prune that number down to be more focussed.

But there are also implementation considerations. Deploying the solution in a real-time decision-making engine (say for credit card transaction authorisations or on-line loan acceptance) requires real-time data, and it can get complicated.

You can have multiple hidden layers. One often works, two or three can be better; it depends on the problem and the input data. You can also have multiple output nodes. This is driven by the problem the neural network is trying to solve.

Let's consider a couple of applications: event prediction and pattern identification.

Event Prediction

Like regression and decision trees, we're trying to predict a future event given observation of the past. Will this customer respond to this offer? What's the likelihood this customer will default on their personal loan? Is this customer about to attrite?

Let's use an example of attempting to predict response to an offer. For a set of inputs about a customer, the network will produce a single output measuring the probability of customer response: at one extreme 0 means absolutely no chance of the customer taking the offer; at the other extreme 1 is a certainty; and there are different degrees of probability in between.

So, how does the neural network develop this capability? The simple answer is that it learns. We train the network to understand what the right answer should be, using historical data about customers who previously did and did not respond to the offer.

All node inputs are assigned a weight, which measures the importance of each input. Using a historical observation, we set the different values on the input nodes, and an output is generated. We already know the actual outcome (its historical data and we know whether the customer responded). The network output is compared with the actual outcome, the error is measured, and nodes are reweighted to compensate for the error. Some become more important, some less so.

And we then use another observation, and another, and another. The neural network keeps reweighting the nodes, getting better and better at predicting the outcome. Eventually, it will stabilise and there won't be further improvement.

All being well, your neural network is now trained and can predict the future. For any set of inputs, it will predict the likelihood of the customer responding to the offer. Now you can test just how good the prediction is by using data it's never seen before. As with other predictive techniques, we use a validation sample.

Pattern Identification
You'll often hear that neural networks are good at identifying patterns, particularly in large data sets. Note that *identifying* is different to *recognising*. The latter is trying to find a pre-determined pattern (maybe a face or a road sign). Pattern identification is looking for something new.

Unlike predictive neural networks, there is no specific target outcome being sought. The network is set loose to find relationships between different inputs, which might be simple (e.g. these two inputs seem to trend together) or complex (e.g. identifying customer clusters).

As each set of inputs is presented, the weights on the various nodes are adjusted to strengthen and weaken the importance. A simple visualisation is to imagine the way you might construct a tally chart. As we tally more data, a pattern gradually emerges and stabilises.

This ability to find something new needs no supervision. It also means that there are no preconceived ideas about what the data represents. Relationships can be discovered and quantified within large amounts of data (including the vast quantities of unstructured data we discussed earlier).

Human experts are needed to assess output and determine whether it represents anything useful or meaningful.

Applications in Banking Analytics

We could use neural networks to replace other, more traditional, analytical techniques. Why continue to use regression or trees?

Neural networks present challenges. The inner workings of the network, and therefore the mechanics of the solution, are obscured by the hidden internal layers. It's impossible to describe those mechanics in recognisable business terms, and that makes people (and some regulators) nervous, particularly where the network is responsible for high profile or high impact decisions. Contrast this lack of transparency with decision trees, where the splits are often easily explained and intuitively make sense.

But the improvements in predictive power can be compelling.

Consider credit card fraud, a $30 billion global exposure (2020 projection), representing around 0.1% of the total transaction volume. That means, for every 1,000 transactions, a single one will be fraudulent. The analytical challenge is significant, not least because of the need to limit:

- False positives (the model predicts fraud, but is wrong); and
- False negatives (the model should have caught a fraud but missed it).

Neural networks offer insights that traditional techniques cannot. You might use unsupervised learning to build a pattern for normal transaction matching, since we could consider a fraudulent transaction *out of pattern*.

Applying similar methodologies to other types of customer fraud and AML monitoring efforts might prove viable since it's also out-of-pattern transaction detection. But what about monitoring for internal fraud? The opportunities are likely limited only by the availability of suitable data to analyse.

Less esoteric applications also exist. Neural nets can identify previously unknown relationships within the data. They can build more effective transformations, adding predictive power to subsequent downstream analysis delivered using traditional techniques.

The use of neural nets and ML continues to grow, and new applications, techniques and methodologies will emerge to further challenge and augment established approaches... and sometimes compel us to change radically.

Analyst versus Machine

So, will we be able to replace our analysts with AI and machine learning any time soon?

Probably not. Almost all today's practical applications for analytics are in supervised learning. For at least the next decade, this is likely to continue, irrespective of the analytical technique being used (remember machine learning covers more than just neural networks).

There will be advances in artificial general intelligence (AGI) to model more generalised human-like approaches to problem solving, rather than the narrow focus of specific applications (like vision or speech). There is no expert consensus on when we might achieve AGI capable machines, but there is agreement it probably remains decades away.

Even assuming a giant leap forward in unsupervised learning techniques, or major improvements in the modelling of general intelligence (at least when applied in a narrow business context), significant barriers to the replacement of analysts remain.

Remember the hard/soft problem types considered earlier? For now, computers like hard problems, not soft ones. In fact, ML solvable problems need to be really hard. That means we need human analysts to deal with anything remotely soft.

But computers are good at scale. So, highly defined problems with a large volume of observations are where a purely computational approach should thrive.

This is represented in Figure 8.2 below. The x-axis represents the soft-hard problem continuum, discussed earlier. The y-axis represents scale; as it increases, we're not increasing complexity, but we are increasing the number of observations and/or the number of potential variables.

There is a class of problems, irrespective of the hardness, where it is of no current benefit to attack using machine learning; there's not enough scale to make the approach economically viable. That's within the human analysis zone in Figure 8.2.

Figure 8.2 Problem Types and Scale

Soft/low is the current human analysis domain, whilst machine learning occupies the hard/high quadrant. This isn't intended to be a precise representation, and delineations will move as technology advances.

The Writing on The Wall

Here are some predictions for analytics over the next decade. First, a few likely business outcomes:

- Domain specific AI solutions will emerge that are "plug-and-play". You probably won't need to invest in internal heavy-lifting AI talent. Packaged solutions will not be cheap, but they'll probably be cheaper than doing it on your own. Global mega-banks will harbour desires to build internal solutions, gambling on delivering a slight edge against the crowd. As with any bet, there will be winners and losers.

- Vertical AI applications will automate call-handling, investment robo-advisors and day-to-day account management (maybe automatically balancing the books or optimising repayments across lending products). Some of this is already starting to be deployed.

- We will make massive and meaningful improvements in money laundering and fraud detection. This will be delivered by AI and DLT in concert.

From a geeky analytics perspective, we can expect:

- Detection of new and unforeseen transforms of the data prior to analysis, significantly improving predictive power. New application packages will free us from the constraints previously associated with the exploration of potential transformations. We used to consider (maybe) less than 100 potentials; we will run to thousands of such assessments.

- Increases in computing power (via the cloud) to further enable significant scale expansion. Analytical techniques such as Random Forest (which automates significant components of the model generation process and tests multiple solutions) were not possible previously and are now commonplace; others will emerge.

- Improvements in automation that will facilitate a large proportion of the advanced analytics delivery processes (particularly data selection and preparation). We'll push 50% automation, but it will ultimately still rely on supervised learning for solution delivery.

  As a result, the role of the analyst will gradually change and become more focussed on the supervision of ML engines, rather than other (more mundane) aspects of the end-to-end execution. Not analyst *versus* machine; more analyst *plus* machine.

- Project definition, requirements evolution, and the process of mapping a soft problem to a sequence of hard tasks will stay human for a considerable time.

- Expert systems, together with more powerful and easily integrated visualisation tools, will remove the need for many more junior analyst roles (primarily supporting the reporting and monitoring tiers of the analytics spectrum).

- Analytical skill in dealing with unstructured data will become more valued. Expertise in text analysis is the fastest and quickest way to unlock value. More generalised fuzzy-logic applications are future opportunities.

- Automation of data governance should dramatically increase (including change detection, accuracy monitoring, validation and audit), such that dedicated support and active management will significantly reduce.

So, the role of the analyst will change. There will be less need for basic analytics delivery and less need for analytics support roles. Which probably doesn't imply fewer analysts, just more interesting roles and more opportunities to add value.

In 2009, Hal Varian (Google's Chief Economist) famously said, "I keep saying that the sexiest job in the next ten years will be statisticians, and I'm not kidding".

I'm thinking maybe it's not statisticians. Maybe data analysts will become the sexiest job of the 21st century.

PART III

APPLICATION AREAS

"The value of an idea lies in the using of it"
Thomas A Edison, Inventor (Feb 1847—Oct 1931)

"Marketing without data is like driving with your eyes closed"
Dan Zarella, Marketing Scientist and author

CHAPTER 9

How to Pick Winners

There will always be relentless demands on analytical resources. A fundamental issue is the pull towards generating more "right here, right now" basic reporting and monitoring, versus the higher value addition of data mining and predictive analytics.

With multiple business demands, priorities, and requests, how do you decide where to expend those precious resources?

This chapter represents the synthesis of 35+ years of managing analytical resources, dealing with client groups, and observing where to derive the highest value from analytics.

Formulating or prescribing "how to pick winners" might seem like a somewhat preposterous ambition. Every business and market is different; customer bases are diverse. But within the uncertainty, noise and fog, there are six observations that have consistently and repeatedly served me well. They might work for you too.

Observation # 1: Focus on the Right Customers

When determining who the right customers are, consider the matrix in Figure 9.1 below. This is based on the Boston Consulting Group market share/growth matrix; using value rather than market share.

The next chapter will consider measures of current and potential value in great detail. The suggested approaches here assume that such measures exist (and are reasonably *accurate* and *trusted* by the business).

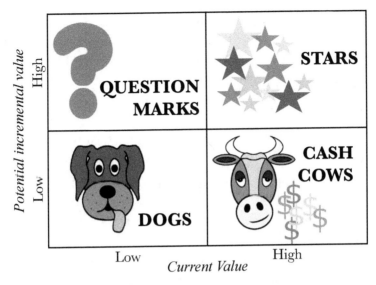

Figure 9.1 Current/Potential Value Matrix

- **Question Marks (low current value; high incremental potential).** Work this group hard to identify how to increase engagement and value. Consider customers at different vintages, their levels of product engagement, historical performance and behaviour, and the servicing model employed.

Converting *Question Marks* into *Stars* or *Cash Cows* is a highly beneficial objective. Understanding why they are *Questions Marks* is an important first step in that process.

- **Stars (high current value; high incremental potential).** Business is already being successfully generated, and there is further untapped potential.

There will be a few "super-traders" here, using products like equities, currency linked deposits, or foreign exchange. There might be other atypical customers here also.

But the *majority* of these customers have regular banking and wealth management needs—which may be currently supported by a skilled manned channel.

There is a need to tread carefully. Customer relationships are working well and delivering value; that's a state worth perpetuating. But there may be important reasons why potential is untapped. For example:

- The customer has deliberately split their business across multiple banks (so limiting opportunities to build additional wallet share).

- The customer is newer vintage and growing their relationship.

- A misalignment of sales resources to customer opportunities. This quadrant is the "sweet spot"; urgently fix the disconnects.

- *Cash Cows (high current value; low incremental potential).* Current performance like *Stars* but with limited further value upside. In many ways, these are your most loyal customers since low incremental potential suggests that you already have a high share of wallet.

This is a "protect and preserve" segment. Customers are contributing substantially to your business success. Do not risk existing revenues and work hard to identify and satisfy any emerging needs.

- *Dogs (low current value; low incremental potential).* Sometimes I see analysts operating down here. When it happens, the analytics engagement model is probably broken; after all, there's no value to be had. There are a couple of possible reasons:

(a) Analytics is struggling to engage with business units and is desperate to take any work to keep busy; or

(b) Analytics cannot get access to the higher priority segments and is being fobbed off with relatively unimportant activities. Fortunately, this happens rarely.

Unlocking value is our primary purpose, and that will not happen in this quadrant. If effort is being spent here, there has been a failure of engagement with the business.

The recommendations here are not intended to be prescriptive; they are a suggested set of approaches. It's also worth remembering that each axis is not a simple high/low binary; it's a continuous range of values from zero to something very much higher. Approaches can be more varied.

Observation #2: Work on Problems that REALLY Matter

Sometimes business heads aren't aware of how much analytics can improve things (and by implication, how sub-optimal current performance might be). Challenging the status quo, generating change and building credibility in the approaches often takes small steps and a protracted timetable... it can be a slow burn impact.

You can accelerate the analytics contribution by allocating analytic effort to work on problems that *really* matter to someone senior. To be frank, the more important the person, the better. What are the problems keeping them awake at night?

Some possibilities:

- Managing provisioning, particularly after the shocks of 2020
- Accelerating incremental revenues to mitigate interest margin pressures
- Fully leveraging opportunities in a large legacy customer base
- Navigating unprecedented competition from non-traditional players

Many such problems are a natural fit for analytics. New insights or solutions (even partial ones) will benefit the business, gain credibility for analytics, and maybe someone senior gets a little more sleep.

At the very least, don't have analytics working on problems that only matter a little.

Observation #3: Focus on the Right Activities

Consider these (highly simplified) components of any marketing campaign:

- Targeting of customers to receive the campaign;
- Creative execution; and
- The offer, including pricing, gifts and promotions.

Traditionally, marketing teams would spend most of their effort on the creative and the offer. The rise of below-the-line initially, and digital more recently, has changed the mix and targeting now gets much more focus—note that targeting includes channel deployment choices and mechanics.

Let's say, for the sake of argument, that nowadays targeting, creative and offer receive equal attention. Look at Figure 9.2, where I've also included my estimates of the actual contribution each activity will likely make to the campaign. Clearly, there's a disconnect.

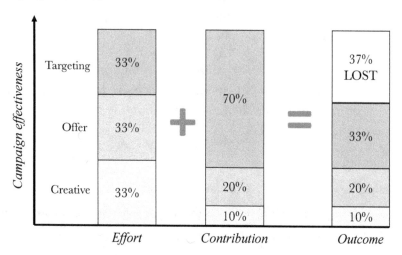

Figure 9.2 Campaign Effectiveness

Creative can only deliver 10% of contribution, so we waste anything above this. In the example above, wastage from creative is 23% (i.e. 33% effort expended less 10% contribution maximum achievable). The situation is similar for the offer component, with 13% of effort wasted.

Targeting represents 70% of the campaign effectiveness, yet only 33% of effort is being spent here, so whilst there is no wastage, there is a loss of opportunity (37% of the total effectiveness in this example).

I recognised this is a simplification, and the return on effort is non-linear and likely diminishing at the margin. I am simply using this as a framework to show:

- how destructive wrongly aligned effort can be, and
- the importance of targeting.

Monoline credit card and direct insurance companies were leveraging this insight back in the nineties, albeit over more limited channels than today —they adopted a fanatical focus on targeting effectiveness.

Nowadays, it's the virtual banks and fintechs that are very focused on targeting. They undertake huge numbers of tests in multiple channels, carefully measuring different aspects of performance to inform and guide the next iteration of testing.

This highlights issues of approach and culture. Can a traditional bank adjust to such a test-focused approach? It's not just about the scale of testing required, it's also about the accurate measurement of results and subsequent course-corrections. We'll discuss the implications in the coming chapters about offers-in-context and CRM.

Observation #4: Time is an Opportunity and a Threat

The graph below in Figure 9.3 shows my estimates of relative contribution again, but this time expanding the targeting aspect a little.

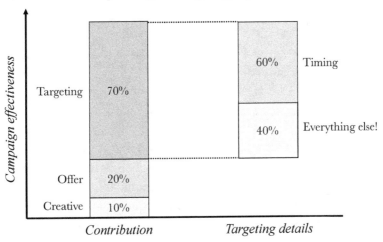

Figure 9.3 Campaign Contribution Revisited

Over the years, I have increasingly realised just how important timing is to the effectiveness of both campaigns and sales activity.

We'll discuss this in more detail later, but for now here's a simple example of how time is a targeting opportunity and a threat. Consider the case where a customer calls your bank to notify you of a change of residential address. The clock is ticking. You have a small window of time to sell them a loan. It's a loan they need for carpets, curtains, wallpaper, paint, a microwave oven, maybe a new bed—all the things you might need when you move home.

Just how small is the window of opportunity? Figure 9.4 shows the situation for one bank I worked with. It shows the response rate to a loan offer for those customers who called in with an address change.

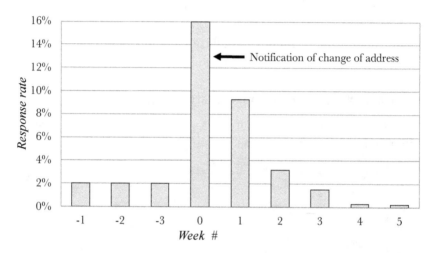

Figure 9.4 Loan Response Rates over Time

The response rate in the pre-notification period is 2%; and then a window where the response rate is significantly higher than normal. However, the notification is a double-edged sword. After the initial period, the response rate quickly drops to a level below the pre-notification norm. This makes sense since the need for a loan has been satisfied (by you or someone else). It will take a considerable amount of time for a new need to develop and the response rate to recover.

This example is a particularly time-sensitive event; others can be less so. Nevertheless, the majority of product offers have a degree of time sensitivity, some of which might be nuanced or subtle. Do I have enough money to pay for it yet? Maybe next year would be better for the family? Should I purchase product X now and product Y later?

For higher levels of time-sensitivity, recognition and offer generation usually requires significant operational and systemic change—it's a very different sales and marketing paradigm. Can you generate an offer one week or one day after observing a customer need? Can you do it in real-time? Can the new offer replace a previously generated offer for something else? Does it need to?

If timing represents 60% of the targeting impact, what else is in the mix?

Communication channel is far and away the most important next level contributor. This is usually much easier for a business to manage and requires a more limited (if any) paradigm shift—particularly if it's a simple choice between one channel and another.

It's essential for any business to optimise channel use. But don't ignore the importance of time—it can be the most important aspect of targeting and is sometimes harder to manage, but the returns can be considerable.

Observation #5: Listen to the Front Line

The folks working in branches, call-centres, anywhere customer facing, are a source of market and customer intelligence. They might also be recipients of analytical output, particularly sales leads.

Create opportunities for analysts to interact and seek their knowledge and experience. They are "at the coal face". They must work with the leads analytics supplies. What's working, and what can be improved?

Knowledge unlocked from the most successful front line sales people can be used to develop offer-in-context targeting. These shared insights will improve the performance of the entire sales team.

The front-line will probably use a lead-management system. What are the challenges and opportunities? Expect an enlightening conversation. At worst, it'll be depressing that all the effort and hard work to generate quality leads is being undermined by poor processes and technology. I've even seen telemarketing teams cross-legged on the floor with pages of leads printed out in front of them. It's eye-opening (and don't get me started on information security implications).

Whatever the situation, analysts need to get out and learn what's going on in day-to-day customer interactions. Just watching the ebb and flow of customers in a branch will give insights into how analytics might support staff better.

It always surprises me how reluctant analysts are to engage the front line. It's a simple and valuable activity; they will become better analysts and better at spotting opportunities for analytics to contribute to business success.

Observation #6: Think Like A Customer

Customers are mostly rational. Often, considering the customer's perspective will deliver a swift solution to a problem. Understand their point of view, develop initial hypotheses, and rapidly test with data and analysis.

This might seem simplistic, but it can be a hard thing to do. We're bankers, trying to understand the needs and motivations of students, single parents, striving mid-market professionals, empty-nesters, and 70-year-old retirees.

You don't need years of experience to do this (although it helps). Empathise for sure, but also understand products, their features and how they're being used; go to customer focus groups; develop a mind's-eye view of different customer segments.

Great analysts think like a customer and nail the correct hypothesis quickly.

Final Comments

Hopefully, these observations will help you pick more winners, but there are no guarantees and no magic wands.

The observations made here are deliberately generic and broad based. The rest of Part 3 will concentrate on specific real-world applications of analytics.

CHAPTER 10

Customer Metrics

When analysing bank customers, there's plenty of data available to quantify the value of each relationship: deposit balances (by type, currency, and tenure), transaction volumes, the number of products held and so on.

But such measures are proxies for true customer value to the organisation, and it's difficult to make cross-product comparisons. Are customers with $10,000 on deposit worth more than customers with a $1,000 loan? How do you rank the value of two groups of credit card customers, one with a high level of spend, the other with a small revolving balance and low spend?

These are thorny problems. As a minimum, any comparison between deposit and loan customers must identify the rough spread and balance for each deposit and loan. It's even more complicated for the credit card example: potentially different interchange rates and different revolving interest rates; what about annual fee payments and late charges?

What is needed is a mechanism aggregating across products to quantify the *total value* of each customer. Without such a personalised assessment of total value, you cannot effectively micro-manage your customer base. Decisions on pricing and offers cannot be optimised, and we're a long way from the relationship recognition we should be striving for.

An unequivocal, accurate and complete measure of customer value is essential. Without it, you're using proxies, and the business is being run on guesswork—highly resolved and well-informed guesswork, but guesswork, nonetheless.

Customer Value

Customer value (CV) should measure the value in individual products held and aggregate to a total.

What does CV deliver?

- A single unambiguous metric for the value of each individual customer relationship. This doesn't remove the need for additional product specific metrics, e.g. a loans initiative needs to measure the number and volume of loans. But CV provides a metric that transcends product or activity specific metrics.

- The fast assessment of portfolio quality and changes over time; particularly useful for different segments. How many customers are low value? How are premium customers performing versus mass?

- The ability to track new vintage total performance. Are revenues developing in line with the assumptions for new acquisition?

- It's easy to determine impacts of portfolio actions and marketing campaigns. Did the card spend stimulation pay for itself? Did the drive for new deposits generate profitable growth?

So, what should be included and what shouldn't? How to define customer value? The construction you use should make most sense to your organisation and its current financial reporting. After all, CV needs to reconcile against a familiar and available number.

Think of customer value as customer level net revenue—or gross income, or gross profit, it's all broadly the same thing, i.e. revenue less the operational expenses associated with generating the revenue.

Revenue Components

Revenue is relatively straightforward: interest charges, commissions, fees, nuisance charges, etc. Don't forget to adjust for refunds and reversals, and reversals of reversals, etc.

The most important revenue lines should already appear on the data warehouse. But there'll probably be gaps for some esoteric products and/or those with small customer numbers. Third party transactions might also be missing. Credits from an insurance company for sales independently made to your customers can be a problem. If revenue is generated from a customer and reported in the business P&L you need to recognise it.

Some data may need more frequent capture. Card receivables or deposits can initially use a monthly number, but daily numbers will significantly improve accuracy.

Expense Components
Whilst revenue lines are mostly available, the warehouse will probably have almost nothing on expenses and won't be receiving any data feeds. This will need effort.

For the customer value calculation, there are two calcuated expenses: rewards points and cost of funds (CoF). Rewards (usually for credit cards only) are often a P&L contra-revenue item but must be calculated for customer value—particularly when attempting to reconcile the calculated value to the P&L reported numbers.

Estimating the expense for credit card rewards should be fairly simple. The Finance department will have the provisioning rate and approach. The approach should be mimicked using the warehouse sales transactions (or whatever else you issue reward points for).

Cost of funds involves a transfer pricing value for different assets and liabilities. New data feeds will be necessary. Finance should be the first place to look, maybe they already have an appropriate consolidated view of the required data. Start with monthly data and then consider the benefits of increased frequency.

Considerations
- Development will require considerable one-time work and will depend on the start point. Plan a staged development. Start with something achievable with existing data, no matter how imperfect.

- Customer value can be calculated monthly for most uses.

- Build the value for each product (e.g. checking); which aggregates to a product group (e.g. CASA); which aggregates to a higher product group (e.g. deposits); which aggregates to the customer.

  Typically, your existing IT systems for product management and financial reporting (with definitions of products and business units) will inform decisions made here about what maps where.

- Prioritise the big products (by customers and by revenue).

- Customer value should reconcile against the P&L. Aggregate customers to some segment (product, proposition, etc) for comparison with the reported P&L—maybe it's credit cards, or Premium Banking, or mortgages.

- As a first milestone, get CV to +/- 20% of the actual P&L numbers. Use plug numbers and realistic estimates when needed.

  The eventual goal should be minimum +/- 10%. Diminishing marginal returns are operating and it gets harder to make progress, but you need to shoot for this with your volume products.

Recognising Credit Losses

Once customer value is sufficiently reconciled, consider credit losses. The data should already exist on the warehouse. Credit losses and recoveries should be separate from customer value. Separation means updates to reflect further recoveries are substantially easier (just update the recoveries field rather than recalculate the customer value).

Figure 10.1 shows a graphical representation of how customer value, as discussed, might be structured for a single customer.

This illustration shows an inherent product grouping and hierarchy where the customer is at the top, and the product totals are at the second level. It doesn't have to be this structure, and we'll discuss product groupings towards the end of this chapter. Use a structure appropriate for your own reporting and reconciliation needs.

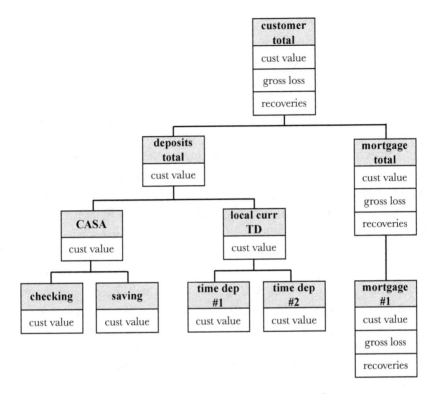

Figure 10.1 Customer Value Aggregation

What about the risk of potential default? Should we bake that into our CV?

Consider a customer at 60 dpd with an 80% likelihood (say) they will crash on through to final default. Does that mean we should write-off 80% of the balance now and adjust the customer value to reflect the loss? Of course not. The customer might cure, maybe become current once more and never trouble us again (unlikely but possible). If they did, we'd need to back out the impact of the potential loss from all previous CV calculations and analysis involving that customer.

If you want to assess the risk aspects of portfolio quality (including risk-adjusted returns and RWA), then do so separately and use customer value as one component of the analysis.

Customer Profitability?

Once you've nailed customer value as a net revenue measure, there's a temptation to push on and generate customer level profitability. Don't be tempted.

Some remaining expenses can be accurately and relatively easily attributed to a customer. But you'll probably have to find the data, or (more likely) find a mechanism to capture it. Other expenses are much more troublesome since a direct relationship to the customer doesn't exist. For example, an individual collections call is easy, but a proportion of a corporate branding exercise is harder. How to allocate branch expenses? Should it be for just retail customers, even though you likely allocate part of that expense to the credit cards business (and maybe others)? And if it is just retail, then should customers pick up an allocation for their domiciled branch only, or the network? And should it be by customers, or accounts, or products, or balances? It's complicated and (honestly) often arbitrary.

Even if the data can be generated and an allocation mechanism agreed, the incremental benefit over and above net revenue is questionable and probably counter-productive. Allocating fixed costs as though they are variable will give a wrong view of performance (of products, segments, customers, and campaigns).

Closing Comments on Customer Value

Developing CV from scratch takes resources, operational system changes and time, maybe as much as a year. But once established, maintenance is usually fairly painless.

The ongoing benefits far outweigh the implementation challenges. Customer value will be critical to your analytics and future CRM efforts.

I will give one simple example of how to apply CV. The graph in Figure 10.2 shows all bank customers rank ordered by CV. Each bar represents around 3% of the total base. I have yet to see a retail bank where value concentration does not occur, and I've seen more extreme concentration than shown below.

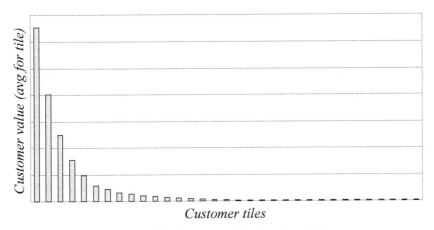

Customer tiles

Figure 10.2 Customers Ranked by Value

The top 10% represents 74% of total value; the top 20% are 90%; and the top 3% is scary. This is fairly typical. Inevitably, such a concentration of value in the top tiers means there is a rather long tail of relatively low value customers.

Considered in the context of the average expense per customer, many customers are underwater. For many banks it's roughly 33% make money, 33% are around breakeven, and 33% are bleeding you.

Another interpretation: the success (or failure) of the business rests with few customers. It might be useful to monitor these customers closely, to check on performance and maybe get someone senior to reach out to them now and again to say, "Thank you".

Asset Customer Potential

It's always useful to have a measure of customer potential. It's not critical in the way customer value must be, but it can be effective for screening customers for wealth management, estate planning, proposition, and even sales channel.

For asset products, estimates of potential are usually less useful (we usually need more firm information for lending purposes) but can be useful to target credit card cobrand propositions and cross-selling retail banking products and propositions. The best source of information for asset customers is often a credit bureau; maybe detailing total lines, products and lenders.

I remember spending three days at an offsite in Singapore with the analytical function heads from every Asia Pacific market. Our objective was to identify opportunities to leverage bureau data; quantifying customer potential was a key requirement. Other opportunities emerged, including:

- Invert the bureau application score to predict future revolving behaviour;

- Recent line assignments can be used to infer current income;

- External lines and recent income can help reverse engineer competitor lending criteria and line assignment.

Important note. Exploitation of bureau opportunities depends on available data, reporting requirements, and bureau conditions of use.

Banking Customer Potential

For general banking customers, identifying customer wealth is a significant step towards quantifying opportunity and identifying share-of-wallet.

Previously, I've tried to identify customer wealth in a few different ways. I'll briefly discuss each. Data availability (internal and external), the overlap of customers between products, and local market circumstances will determine the appropriateness of each.

Approach #1: Using Income Estimation

The initial hypothesis was that we could model income across the total banking customer base. Income would then be used to estimate wealth.

Banks rarely capture income for typical banking customers. But we capture it for most asset customers (including credit cards, PIL and mortgage); we can use the overlap population to model income. Payroll accounts clearly give you income information, and if the population is large enough, this might be used as a further analytical dataset.

In highly simplified terms, you need to find a population where information is available on age, occupation, gender and income, and asset products will typically deliver this from application forms.

The logic to build the income estimation goes like this:

- Men earn more than women; unfair but usually true.

- Occupations will rank order, e.g. driver vs bank manager vs pilot.

- Typically, income will increase with age, at least during early career.

- So, combinations of gender/occupation/age will rank order income.

- Therefore, income can be derived when generic banking customer information has gender, occupation and age. Accuracy is high.

- Analytical note: Beware outliers, there are often a few extreme observations and they can mess things up here.

Once we'd built the income estimation, we needed to model wealth. This proved to be a real challenge. We thought all we needed to do was apply basic assumptions about expenses and savings accumulation; wealth would magically pop-out. We failed spectacularly. Wealth accumulation was influenced by many more factors than income alone. With hindsight, I should have simply looked at my personal circumstances to realise the possibility of this outcome.

But at least we built a really good income estimator.

Approach #2: Using observed product behaviours
This time, we would go at it from the outset. No more intermediate steps, we'd make the jump straight to light-speed, and crack wealth estimation using observations of customer behaviour.

The logic was sound. We could see so much data: incoming deposits, balance accumulation, diversification into different products (particularly wealth management including equities, mutual funds), and we had all the demographic data too. We thought we had built an excellent model.

Well, it wasn't a complete disaster... only a partial one. It worked spectacularly well when we had a high proportion of customer wallet, but performance degraded as wallet share declined. Unfortunately, many customers used multiple banks, and whilst we were often the lead bank, we still didn't have a complete enough picture.

Fortunately, we carefully tested the results with a few customers and relationship managers. Problems were identified early. Rightly, we dumped this approach completely; there were too many key customers where the model was plain wrong.

Approach #3: Using on-us and off-us observations

Engagement with the front-line relationship managers (RMs) had taught us that what they really wanted was a way to identify missed opportunities i.e. affluent customers already in the portfolio, but who could do more.

We redefined the analytical task to focus on the identification of the highest levels of affluence. We needed an indicator to flag super affluent, affluent and emerging affluent customers.

In order of importance, the four important variables used were:

1. **Home value.** The home you live in is highly predictive of affluence. You may be the mortgage lender, or mortgage data might be available externally (Hong Kong has the Land Registry as a source). Whether it's rented or owned is not important; high purchase value also equates to a high rental value.

   You might not have provided the mortgage, but you might still see the payment. It'll be the largest monthly out-going from the customer account and not varying much per month.

   By the way, if the largest monthly transaction is USD 1,234.56 then it's a mortgage; if the payment is USD1,250.00 it's probably rent.

   Other smart filters can be applied to improve the accuracy of your estimates, mostly dependent on available market data.

2. **Total relationship balance**. Not the current TRB, but the largest TRB identified over recent years. And it shouldn't be a short-term spike.

3. **Income**. Ok, I failed previously on using income to determine wealth, but this time around the analytical brief was different. Now I'm trying to highlight potential missed opportunities.

   A sneaky Hong Kong tactic is for banks to offer significant benefits for tax payments made via credit cards, e.g. cash rebates, reward points, interest-free loans. The sole purpose of these efforts appears to be determining the customer tax obligation and therefore income. And you don't have to do it every year or even offer it to the whole base, just to those customers where you think it might add a valuable insight.

4. **Credit card spending**. Another useful proxy if you have a reasonable overlap between customer bases. High monthly spending, the pattern of merchant categories and high repayment rates are predictive of affluence.

I have excluded two other criteria due to commercial sensitivity. But there should be enough here to give you the basic building blocks for how you might construct an affluence indicator.

Figure 10.3 shows how the variables previously discussed are used to identify different levels of affluence. This approach has been used in a number of markets and adapted to reflect external data availability.

The final thresholds for each variable were decided in partnership with the front-line customer facing relationship managers. It was trial and error. The tighter the thresholds, the smaller the number of opportunities. What do the front-line need?

Up-front agreement was that super-affluent should not exceed 2% of the total base and the total number of affluent should be around 20%.

We haven't discussed customer age previously, but it's needed to help identify the emerging affluent.

This is not analytically complex, although it might include modelled components. It is analytically nuanced and subtle, requiring intensive interaction with, and contribution from, the end-user community.

Criteria		Super Affluent	Affluent	Emerging Affluent	Mass
	Property value (from mortgage or rental)	>US1.8M	>USD1.0M	>USD500k; age<40	All others
OR	*CONFIDENTIAL*				
OR	*CONFIDENTIAL*				
OR	Maximum 3 month average TRB in the last 24 months	>USD700k	>USD150k	>USD75k; age<40	All others
OR	Annual income	>USD700k	>USD150k	>USD75k; age<40	All others
OR	Monthly credit card spend and payment > 90%	>USD7,500	>USD3,000	>USD1,500; age<40	All others
Proportion of customer base		**1.8%**	**12.4%**	**6.0%**	**79.8%**

Figure 10.3 Customer Affluence Tagging

Here's how it works:

- Start with Super Affluent. If a customer hits any of the criteria, then they are tagged.

- If they don't fulfil any of the Super Affluent criteria, try the Affluent.

- Continue until all criteria have been tested. If the customer drops all the way through, they should be tagged mass market.

This approach was incredibly popular with the front-line. It was simple to understand. They had contributed to the criteria selection and cut-offs, and it was successful in flagging potential opportunities within the portfolio.

Product Holdings: The Good, the Bad, and the Ugly

Before we close out this chapter on customer metrics, I want to discuss a specific metric every bank uses: average product holdings per customer.

Again, this is not an analytically complex issue, it's trivial. But it can speak to the organisational readiness to exploit analytics. If you can't correctly answer something as simple as "How many products do customers hold, on average?" then you've got problems, most likely of organisational culture rather than data availability.

In my experience, product holdings information can be defined in three distinct ways.

The Good. Product holdings are a mechanism for tracking the underlying engagement of customers, using a common-sense definition of what constitutes a product. This means:

- The organisation has a target for engagement (and product holdings).

- There is a commitment to striving for the target with specific actions.

- The metric is seen as strategic.

The Bad. Product holdings are applied inconsistently. Maybe the definitions are deficient, or there is an inconsistent strategic application.

The Ugly. Product holdings are for PR purposes to claim a high level of customer engagement. Typically, it means product holdings are artificially inflated, and there's no real strategy to cross-sell or deepen.

A word of caution. It has been my experience that there is a direct correlation between the commitment to a strategic use of product holding and a determination to embrace analytics. If you are working in a bad or ugly environment, think through the implications. Progress in building analytics will probably be slow, and frustration will be high.

With that in mind, here's guidance about how to measure product holdings and how to benchmark whether you're good, bad or ugly.

A Suggested Approach

A product should only count once. If a customer has four local currency time deposits (LCY TD), even if they have different durations, it counts as one product. However, a foreign currency time deposit (FCY TD) would count as an additional product, but only once.

One possible structure is shown in Figure 10.4 below. The fundamentals of this framework were developed with my old friend, colleague, and über-analyst Marc Giretto, over 20 years ago; it still has enormous relevance today.

There are five product families, seven product groups and 25 unique products. Tailor a similar approach to your own circumstances and needs. Conversations about where to place investment linked insurance are always animated.

You can report product holdings at each one of these levels; but the critical single measure is the 25 individual products.

SPEND	LEND		TRANSACT	WEALTH MGMT		PROTECT
Card	**Loan**	**Mortgage**	**CASA**	**Deposits**	**Investments**	**Insurance**
Credit card	Revolving	Revolving	Current acct	LCY TD	Unit Trusts	Credit
Charge card	Installment	Installment	Savings	FCY TD	Str notes	General
Revolving	Secured		Checking	Unfixed	Bonds	Travel
Installment	Port Finance				Equities	Life
					Inv linked ins	

Figure 10.4 Product Holdings

Conclusions

The topics covered in this chapter aren't analytically sexy or advanced. But the relevance and value to the business is incredibly high.

I'm not a fan of the business maxim "What gets measured, gets managed". The implication is that if it's measured, then it has management attention and will be actively managed. But it says nothing about whether you're measuring the right things in the right way, or whether that management is appropriate, or whether the measurement is making a difference to the management approach (maybe through driving change or correcting inefficiency).

The right measurement is critical to any business. It helps to determine the optimal deployment of business resources, capital, and effort. For analytics, it is also necessary to quantify and prove business contributions. As a minimum, customer value and product holdings should be part of your measurement approaches.

We will repeatedly return to the subject of measurement during our further consideration of application areas for analytics. We should start with measuring campaign effectiveness.

CHAPTER 11

Measuring Campaign Effectiveness

Integral to any discussion of analytical application areas is the consideration of how we measure effectiveness.

We can attribute some element of effectiveness to just "knowing". The knowledge acquisitions from January now have an average balance of US$12,345; the knowledge attrition has reduced from 8% to 6%; the knowledge 43% of general banking customers have been cross-sold a credit card, and their spend volume is 27% higher than card only holders.

But translating this knowledge into a measure of effectiveness needs activity that can be tracked. We might want to increase the average balance from US$12,345 to US$23,456, or reduce attrition further, or increase card cross-sell penetration from 43% to 50%. Now we have goals and we need to plan activities to reach those goals. We can measure the impacts of these activities.

In fact, all marketing campaigns attempting to drive a specific customer behaviour are the ideal opportunity to apply measurement. The behaviour being driven might be response to an offer, or increasing spend, or building deposits, or something else entirely. We need to measure the effectiveness of our attempts to drive these behaviours.

Performance Lift

Analysts will often talk about *performance lift* (the amount something has increased). The lift compares performance between one state and another. Maybe it's different time periods, maybe it's the application of improved targeting. Different types of lift are shown in Figure 11.1.

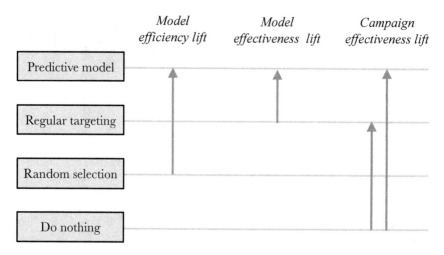

Figure 11.1 Different Types of Performance Lift

We discussed *model efficiency lift* with predictive model Gains charts and graphs, where model performance is being compared against a random sample of the underlying customers. This random sample is the baseline which measures "if we made the offer to all the customers, what would the performance be?". Comparison with that baseline is the traditional way to evaluate the efficiency of predictive models. But it doesn't help in quantifying the value to the organisation since we don't typically make random offers to all customers.

The true value and contribution should compare the model performance against the regular targeting used historically, and which is presumably being replaced by the model targeting. That's the *model effectiveness lift*. This should become part of the measured value contribution from advanced analytics; for any analytical application it's perfectly reasonable to lay claim to impacts for a protracted period (not in perpetuity, but maybe for 18 months). Any subsequent model should be measured against the performance of the old model prior to decommissioning.

Finally, the *campaign effectiveness lift* is used to show the performance of the campaign. A customer might perform actions without being targeted with an offer or inducement. Therefore, to measure the performance of the campaign, we also need to measure the performance of "doing nothing".

Measuring "do nothing" might sound weird, so let's demonstrate using an example. Assume new customers booked in January will build their average balances from $12,345 in March to $23,456 in June. This is part of their continued engagement and the setup of their new banking relationship. If we undertake any additional balance development campaigns to target these customers, then we cannot assess campaign performance based on the simple balance growth. We should not take credit for something that would have happened anyway.

What to Measure?

Specific campaign objectives should inform the primary measurement. If the goal is new accounts, then measure that. If it's new funds, then measure that.

There are a few caveats:

- When targeting analytics for asset products, we are usually concerned with applications, rather than approvals. This allows more flexibility in targeting deployment.

- For clarity, "response" here is defined as "sale made" rather than an "expression of interest". That doesn't mean that measuring expressions of interest is not important.

- There may be multiple steps in the sales process that need to be measured. For example, an email needs to be: (1) opened and read (*open rate*); (2) a link clicked (*click-through rate*); and (3) an application completed and submitted (*application rate*).

    Every step needs measuring, trying to understand why the number of customers drops at each stage and so improve the end-to-end success. For email, you should also monitor: unsubscribe rate, forward rate, bounce rate, etc.

- Channels will probably exhibit different levels of conversion from initial expressions of interest to sales made. Measuring sales focuses on the clear and unequivocal business outcome. This is important when cross-channel comparisons of effectiveness are being made.

Control Groups and Statistical Significance

The performance of "doing nothing" is measured by isolating a group of customers as a no contact *control group*. The composition of this group must be exactly the same as the target group being used for the campaign. If we are targeting customers booked in January for balance development, then some of them should be isolated as a control group.

If the target is "males", then don't use "females" for the control. If the target is the top 10% of model-predicted customers, then don't use the next 10% as the control. The populations must be *exactly* the same otherwise any comparison is flawed.

Campaign effectiveness is the impact of campaign performance less control group performance.

Part of any evaluation must consider the *statistical significance* of the results. Significance measures the likelihood of the results being repeatable and not based on chance alone. If you have a significance of 95% then 95 times out of a hundred, the results would be similar. I'm not going into the technical details here. Suffice to say that larger samples generate higher results significance; and significance also increases with larger response volumes.

Two typical problems can emerge:

- No thought is given to significance when designing the campaign, which leads to insufficient responses and therefore inconclusive results.

- Significance is also necessary in the control group results, which requires reasonably large numbers of potential contacts to be excluded from the promotion/campaign. That's not normally an attractive option for the product owner, particularly if those customers are high potential and goals are being chased.

The importance of significance testing cannot be avoided so embrace it, live with it and make sure results are as bullet proof as realistically and practically possible.

I know that statisticians will probably roast me for the following observations, but:

- Gut feel from a subject-matter expert can transcend statistical shortcomings in the sample or results, but the expert isn't a miracle worker and does need *something* to work with.

- The greater the difference between the test and control group results, the more likely the results are to be accurate.

- A directionally correct result (e.g. it's up when it should be up) is often more useful than an absolute measure (e.g. it's up by 12.3%). This can be useful when you see the same effects from multiple tests.

To further compound my sins and statistical damnation:

- For high rigor aim for 150 responses per test group or cell. This can be difficult, e.g. 1% response means 15,000 customers in each cell, including the control.

- It's often more realistic to aim for *at least* 50 responses for any test cell. Take great care interpreting anything below that. It is possible, considering the observations made above, but tricky.

I'm likely to be flamed for these observations, but there needs to be some business reality. We are often *severely* constrained by customer volumes, budgets, and time.

Occasionally, I have had the luxury of large samples and subsequent high confidence in results. But most of the time, it's 20 or 30 responses in each of four or five cells, compared to a control of about 50 responses. It's not ideal; volumes are low; but I still need to work with what I've got and make recommendations for the next phase of activity. It's inevitably a judgement call.

As results build over multiple months, aggregating similar results delivers increasing robustness and confidence.

Test and Learn Cycle

The continuous enhancement of campaigns can be structured. Figure 11.2 shows the approach. Use this cycle to test major changes in targeting or approaches. It can also test more subtle nuances of the targeting by changing specific attributes.

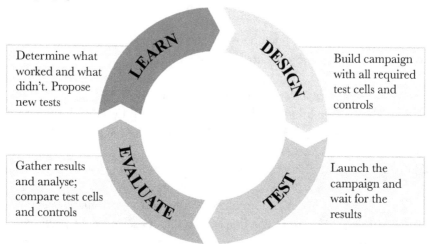

Determine what worked and what didn't. Propose new tests

Build campaign with all required test cells and controls

Gather results and analyse; compare test cells and controls

Launch the campaign and wait for the results

Figure 11.2 The Test and Learn Cycle

Head-to-head tests are often called A/B testing. Two different approaches are being tested (unsurprisingly, called A and B). You could also test C, D, or many variants. The target population is randomly allocated to each different offer and head-to-head competition determines "the winner".

One specific type of A/B testing is called "Champion/Challenger". The current targeting approach is the champion. Against this, one or more challengers are tested i.e. different targeting approaches for the same offer. If a challenger wins, it becomes the new champion. Next cycle, propose new challengers.

Attribute testing is more subtle and usually needs careful design. Consider the following requirements for an example campaign:

- Test four price points: A (most attractive to the customer) to D
- Test with/without introductory promotional offer
- Test targeting males versus females
- Minimum cell size to generate a suitable response volume is 20,000

	MALES		FEMALES	
	with promo	without promo	with promo	without promo
A	20,000	20,000	20,000	20,000
B	20,000	20,000	20,000	20,000
C	20,000	20,000	20,000	20,000
D	20,000	20,000	20,000	20,000
Total	80,000	80,000	80,000	80,000

Figure 11.3 Multiple Attribute Test Design

Figure 11.3 shows a campaign design where every combination of attributes is tested. There are situations where you might want to limit the number of targets; maybe there are budget constraints (on cost of contact or cost of promotion), or the number of available targets is limited.

There are some highlighted cells that could possibly be removed with no likely impact on results (representing 37% of the total). We could test all price points only for females without the promotion and use the A and D price points for the other columns to estimate the missing cells.

In this example, we only tested three attributes, but it can get way more complicated.

Your new understanding of test/control and champion/challenger will serve you well over the next few chapters where we consider the application of analytics in detail.

CHAPTER 12

Lifecycle Analytics: Acquisition

Every customer has a lifecycle, describing the various stages they go through in their relationship with your organisation. The remaining discussion about the application of analytics will take place within that lifecycle framework. Our customer lifecycle has four stages:

- *Acquisition*. All the work the bank did to attract the customer; from the push of sales and marketing, to the pull of branding and location.

- *Engagement*. The early stages of the relationship, the first transactions and interactions; so important for setting the longer-term nature, pattern and scope of activities.

- *Development*. The customer's longer-term pattern of behaviour, where we are ensuring product needs are appropriately identified and met.

- *Retention*. Engagement and development are obviously important for ensuring sustained customer loyalty. But sometimes, things unravel, and sometimes the customer will leave. Retention tries to anticipate customer attrition and provide mechanisms attempting to mitigate it.

This isn't rocket science. Our ambitions are simple:

Getting the right customers
    ... developing them
        ... and keeping them.

There are many opportunities to apply analytics at each phase. This chapter deals with acquisition.

General Observations

More than any other part of the customer lifecycle, acquisition is where marketers get to deploy their full arsenal. Acquisition here applies to *new-to-bank* customers. So, cross selling across consumer segments (e.g. cards to general banking customers, or general banking to mortgage-only) isn't acquisition, it's an aspect of existing customer deepening efforts.

The power of the brand (including awareness, trust and reputation), public relations, sponsorship activity, the branch footprint (it sometimes still matters) and existing familial relationships; all contribute to delivering new-to-bank acquisition.

But from an analytical perspective, we need to focus on *harder* activities where we can clearly measure effectiveness—such as various forms of promotions, and particularly prospecting.

It is possible to apply measurement discipline to the softer activities, but it involves a bit of guesswork and a structured approach. Typically, you need to look for additive impacts. If your regular "walk-in" business (i.e. business generated with no associated campaigns or sales/marketing actions) is X accounts and during a period of above-the-line (ATL) activity that rate becomes X+Y, then you can attribute Y to the incremental ATL activity.

There are a few things to be aware of with this approach:

- It is far easier to attribute an acquisition to an action when you're building momentum and adding new activities. As activities are discontinued, residual impacts can make reading the situation difficult, e.g. direct mail creates response weeks after initial delivery; the increase of awareness and brand recognition from a television commercial might have impacts months later.

- Many softer activities are difficult to cost justify when hard metrics (new accounts opened, balances booked, etc) are applied. There are often intangible or unquantifiable impacts. And there may also be a contribution to the regular walk-in number of X (whether through improving the brand perception, raising awareness, or something else).

- It can be difficult to identify the regular walk-in X... after all, when is there ever a period of no sales or marketing activity?

  This isn't necessarily an issue. Concentrate on the additive impacts. If it's a big multichannel campaign, introduce each media separately to identify the specific performance impact each element contributes (remembering to recognise potential lagging implications).

So, the effectiveness of some activities is relatively difficult to measure. But others are much easier; let's start with digital acquisition.

Digital Acquisition

There are a few choices on how to use digital, but there are really only two that deliver volume: search and display. The landscape is somewhat wider, but note:

- Email is a direct channel and, for acquisition, should be viewed in much the same way as direct mail (albeit usually at a lower level of performance).

  There is one important distinction. With email it is relatively easy to determine the best offer delivery days/times to maximise open and click-through rates (CTR)—"never on Sundays and Mondays" is usually a good place to start, but it can vary by product and audience.

- Social media has been successfully used for raising awareness, brand building and the monitoring of consumer sentiment and brand health. It can be more problematic as an acquisition source—particularly when the full costs are recognised.

  Whether using display ads, sponsored content or influencers, effectiveness must be fully tracked through to new accounts.

Search

For many consumers, the start point for the discovery of potential financial service providers is the search engine query. Analytics applied to *search engine optimisation* (SEO) will help increase the rankings of those results.

There's plenty of advice, expertise and tools available to help. Google publishes some good guidance on how to improve rankings, but the precise algorithm used remains hidden. But this is not a black art, it's a science and much is derivable by experimentation and experience.

However, for all the effort to improve ranking, there are some stark realities about click-through rates:

- Organic (i.e. not paid for) results decline precipitously with ranking. 20-35% of all possible click-through goes to #1; and 60-70% for the top 5 combined.

- The lower-ranked results on the first page (those that require some scrolling to get to) are low single digit CTR. And the second page of results is a desert wasteland for most acquisition.

- Sponsored results and rich content (primarily *snippets* and *local packs* in Google jargon) will impact CTRs by as much as 50%, because when they appear, they (a) draw immediate attention; and, (b) drop the physical position of the organic results further down the page.

Your inclusion in rich content can be influenced as part of a broader SEO approach. For sponsored links, you need to put your hand in your pocket.

Sponsored links appear at the top of the page and the fight for ownership can be fierce, reflecting the importance of the physical position on the page and the competitive nature of your market.

Pick *long-tail keywords* (search queries with 4 or more words). Longer queries avoid competition, reduce cost, and increase focus on your areas of competitive strength—if you believe you are "the best bank for equity trading in Singapore" then own it.

Display
Display advertisements allow you to present your brand and message to consumers visiting third party sites. Ad networks consolidate advertising space, so you don't have to negotiate with individual sites (Google's Display Network claims over 2 million sites).

Things to consider:

- Limit automatic placement, which uses algorithms to place ads on sites that are considered most relevant. Exert control and get focus by using manual placement.

- Display gives opportunities for rapid cycle testing. Exploit this through the extensive use of copy and creative variations.

- Remarketing gives strong results. Every visitor to your site picks up a cookie, and then your ad can appear when they visit other (possibly unrelated) sites.

- Programmatic advertising allows more precision in your targeting (improving the relevance, CTR, and/or cost-effectiveness of your ads) but involves more complexity. If you're struggling to find incremental performance improvements from regular ad network use, then programmatic might be the next level solution.

Of course, the rise of ad blockers and browser functionality to disable cookies is impacting opportunities. Conversely, harnessing AI might deliver new targeting mechanisms that broaden the targeting landscape.

Developing Digital
Many banks have yet to fully exploit digital marketing for new customer acquisition. To date, that hasn't really been a major issue, since traditional approaches have continued to deliver the required accounts and balances.

But consumer habits continue to evolve, and the importance of digital acquisition will inevitably grow—particularly as banks increasingly embed offers into third-party interactions (e.g. retailer internet point of sale loan offers).

A couple of final observations on digital acquisition:

- You can use third parties to get digital acquisition activities started, there's plenty of deep expertise out there; you can learn whilst you build internal capabilities.

- The importance of rapid tracking for digital activities cannot be overstated. Performance measurements should inform a feedback mechanism to adjust bids based on device type, location, scheduling.

So, what about non-digital, those traditional approaches that have continued to hold up well?

Direct Marketing Targeting

Direct approaches (like mail and email) rely on sources of external data from commercial list brokers, third-parties or partner organisations. Where targeting data is available, predictive modelling can be used to target smaller volumes for increased response.

Cold-call telemarketing is (very nearly) a thing of the past—impacted by national "do not call" registers, call-blocking software and/or poor returns.

Quality direct mail—using a sophisticated pack, strong messaging and good targeting—has never fallen out of favour and performance has typically remained good. Indeed, the tech savvy millennials, so adept at quickly scanning through digital content, may well be snagged by the tangible, touchy-feel of a well put together mailing pack.

Consumers are far less tolerant of junk mail today and relevance matters more than ever. As mass approaches have declined, niche partner sources of leads have gained increased importance. Particularly so, where an offer can leverage an affinity or exploit aspects of the partner's relationship with the customers (possibly through reward points or crossover privileges). These also represent typical opportunities for offers in context.

A Note on Asset Products

For anyone engaged in larger volume direct approaches for asset products, predicting response is only half the battle; approvals also need to be considered.

Remember:

- Typically, response and approval inversely correlate. As the response rate goes up, the approval rate goes down. It's possible to build a net conversion model, factoring in both response and approval. I've not had much success with this approach; there's a significant loss of flexibility in testing at the margins of acceptable response and approval.

- Pre-approved offers to high net worth individuals can work if the proposition is sufficiently compelling. But credit bureau screened pre-approval becomes increasingly uneconomic as you descend the risk spectrum, i.e. the screening delivers a smaller proportion of acceptable leads as risk increases.

- *Contingent pre-approval* is a convenient mechanism to unlock the response benefits of full pre-approval without really committing (the approval is contingent on something, like bureau screening or income level). However, it is of questionable transparency.

Other Acquisition Approaches

Sales Force Planning

In Asia particularly, direct selling remains popular, and using analytics to target geographical areas for the sales force is effective.

I've generated a list of *revolver malls* in a few Asian cities, i.e. shopping locations that are more likely to generate cardholders who will roll their balances. The approach is rudimentary: identify the transactions in each mall, then attribute between transactors and revolvers. There's not huge separation; nevertheless, it will significantly improve the average odds of attracting revolvers (if that's the ambition).

Obviously, a similar approach might target more affluent spending malls, retailers, or geographical areas.

For location analysis where you want to define specific areas, you are usually hostage to data availability and its geographical resolution—which varies hugely by country. With the right data it's possible to build detailed branch footprints and quantify market penetration, identify new branch locations, and highlight opportunities for network rationalisation or consolidation.

Member-get-Member

Not much analytics is needed to target member-get-member offers to existing customers. But if MGM is used extensively, there'll likely be customers *gaming* the system, e.g. friend opens a new account, customer gets rewarded, friend closes account. Analytically scope the extent of the abuse; take action given sufficient cause.

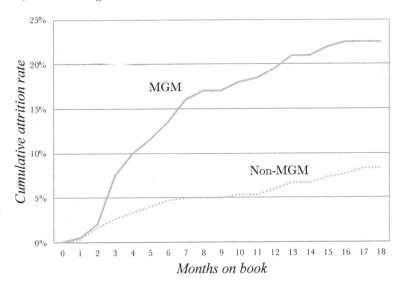

Figure 12.1 MGM versus Non-MGM Attrition

The relative quality of MGM acquired accounts can sometimes be a problem, both in terms of higher attrition and lower average balances—both evidence of customer *gaming* behaviour. In the attrition example shown in Figure 12.1, new retail banking customers, acquired via MGM, had to keep their account open for a minimum of two months to qualify for the acquisition premium. The gaming impacts are obvious.

Miscellany

There are obviously other sources of acquisition—including partners, distributors and other third parties who are often leveraged for new mortgage, personal loan, and instalment plans.

These will probably have robust financial tracking to facilitate commission payments and the like. Nevertheless, treat such acquisitions like any other and thoroughly evaluate performance.

Acquisition Evaluation

Acquisition should be tracked at three different levels:

- Through-the-door (TTD)[2] tracking should cover basic new-to-bank acquisition volumes. The more challenging the acquisition goals, the greater the importance of monitoring TTD run-rates.

- Evaluating the effectiveness of each campaign, activity and initiative, to determine *relative* performance. Without such an assessment it is impossible to optimise spend across different media or activities.

- Periodic longer-term performance review is also required. All acquisition has account performance and profitability assumptions that inform the budgets. These need to be verified occasionally.

There's a lot of analysis associated with this level of tracking. To deliver what is required will probably take process redesign, standardisation of metrics and automation of reporting. Develop a roadmap and a gradual roll-out schedule.

Through-the-Door Tracking

Let's start with the obvious: track all through-the-door acquisition volumes. That includes campaigns, direct sales, walk-ins, internet, everything. Start with daily tracking for large campaigns and anything digital; weekly or monthly for everything else—and get faster from there.

For tracking, we're primarily interested in new customers rather than accounts. For asset products, where there is a credit approval process, you should be tracking applications *and* approvals (although these are probably different groups of customers, e.g. Monday approvals might have been applications from days ago). Highlight daily, month-to-date, quarter-to-date, year-to-date versus target... anything that keeps everyone focused on the volume goals and run-rates.

---

[2] Something of a misnomer given the small proportion of new customers who actually walk through the door

Assign a source code to everything; this will attribute each acquisition to an activity. The usefulness of any evaluation is directly linked to the quality and completeness of the source coding.

When you're designing your campaigns and activities, think about how the results will be tracked and what source codes are required to support that tracking. Typical problems include:

- Not enough source code resolution, so multiple activities are allocated the same code (and subsequently can't be tracked separately).

- Poorly designed data-entry processes, making it difficult to identify the correct source code. *This happens remarkably often.* Audit for correctness and fix process defects.

Acquisition Effectiveness
Tracking the volume of applications is the first step. There needs to be a subsequent assessment of effectiveness. Was the acquisition cost per customer on target? Was the intended acquisition volume achieved?

Some acquisition is impossible to cost; for example, an unattributed branch walk-in, or an internet application with no identifiable source. This forms part of your background run-rate new-to-bank acquisition.

Digital activities usually have very transparent costs (at least if you are using pay-per-click) so it's straightforward to adjust strategies based upon results; intra-day if required. It should also be relatively easy to identify the precise cost of each new customer.

Activities might have more complicated cost structures, including customer gifts or incentives, sales commissions, media, advertising agency fees, production costs, etc. When considering what to include, remember that the primary objective is not to attribute all costs; it is to make fair comparisons between different activities, e.g. direct mail campaign versus social media banner ad versus direct sales event versus radio ad.

For asset products, there's a delay waiting for customers to be approved (which might be multiple weeks from the receipt of application). Tracking should include approvals, declines, suspended, cancelled, etc.

Performance Monitoring

Acquisitions are made in the expectation that the customer will deliver a specific level of return. We should therefore check those assumptions from time to time.

Performance tracking shouldn't stop at the point of acquisition. Tracking engagement activities during early vintage is also important and often unveils problems with specific acquisition campaigns or approaches.

Months-on-books (MOB) is the standard way to show customer vintage; a customer at MOB 6 has been with the bank for six months. Use MOB reporting of customer value, balances, spend, activation rates, fraud, and delinquencies. Add others appropriate to the business.

Let's be realistic here. Most businesses are running multiple campaigns over numerous channels across many months. Tracking each activity (for MOB 1, 2 and beyond) is probably an insane goal for most, at least initially.

So start simple and build out. The granularity of reporting doesn't have to start high. As a minimum, maybe track all new bookings for January, and then February, then March, and so on. Over time, use automation to add more details and scale.

General Observations on Effectiveness

1. Gift/premium analysis. I've seen some spectacular retail banking acquisition premiums... and spectacular attrition rates that go with them. Don't reward just for opening an account. Make the reward contingent on a behaviour, such as bringing in a specific level of balances.

   The meta-data (details about the campaign) are likely to be incomplete and in need of attention.

2. Watch the opt-out rates for new customers; they may reveal potential issues. This can be a function of the application process/design, the target audience, or some other wildcard.

3. A sudden increase in acquisition volume can lead to a deterioration in account quality; often a function of *sales push* rather than *customer pull*. Without an expansion of the overall potential universe, it's possible you're "scrapping the bottom of the barrel" as you push for more volume.

A further implication is that unless such accounts are highly self-servicing, existing processes and resources can be stressed.

4. Beware promotional rates at acquisition. Stick rates (the amount that survives the transition to the standard rate at the expiry of the promotion) can be a problem.

It's not much of an issue for deposits since the spread between the promotional bonus rate and funding rate is usually not extreme— and we gain some intelligence on customer wealth.

It can be a major problem for credit card balance transfers (BT). The economics of all promotional BT acquisition strategies depend on the BT rate versus cost of fund (CoF) and the ultimate stick-rate. I've got a few horror stories (which unfortunately can't be shared), especially when you make offers to high net worth/high line/low risk customers with no requirement to pay down an external balance. These folks can seriously game you.

You need to keep on top of this analytically, continually monitoring how sticky the promotional balances are because once your rates are below CoF, profitability can unravel quickly.

Decisioning on Asset Products

The approval process should be considered as a component of acquisition and, whilst this is primarily the domain of Risk Management, there are a couple of things that are worth keeping an eye on.

- Analyse line assignments for unexpected behaviours. For more affluent (and less credit needy) customers, a low line assignment can dramatically increase inactivity and never-active rates. This makes intuitive sense: why bother carrying more plastic with a low line?

Conversely, a high line assignment can drive other issuer plastic out of such wallets, thus increasing the share of spend.

- Periodically review the *decline waterfall*. Applications are declined for failing myriad criteria, as shown in the mock-up in Figure 12.2. It shows the decline reason and volume on each line. In this example, the total decline rate is 52.1%.

Verify the reasons make sense. Usually, criteria are easily added (as credit quality deteriorates) and less easily removed (as quality improves). If there are triggers for tightening, make sure that there are also triggers for loosening.

	Applications	Declines	%age of total	Cum % declined
Application score fail	19,723	7,021	35.6%	35.6%
Undesirable occupations	12,702	253	1.3%	36.9%
On-us write-off	12,449	188	1.0%	37.8%
Fraud score fail	12,261	173	0.9%	38.7%
Bureau score fail	12,088	2,469	12.5%	51.2%
Off-us write-off	9,619	321	0.9%	52.1%
etc				
Total	9,298	10,425		52.1%

Figure 12.2 Application Waterfall

This example is in chronological order of applying each criterion. Check that you go to bureau after all internal screening. Why pay for bureau data on applications that would be dumped out by some other internal criteria?

During decisioning there will be *pended* applications i.e. those that can't be fully decisioned, often because documentation is incomplete. They're a marketing opportunity, but they age quickly. It doesn't take long for them to be forever in the cancelled pile. Tell the customer quickly of the outstanding requirements and treat it as a marketing communication rather than a credit operations follow-up. Test the time sensitivity.

CHAPTER 13

Lifecycle Analytics: Banking

The central components of the customer lifecycle are engagement and development, which involves new customers at the start of their banking relationship through to longer-term behaviours and the ongoing identification and fulfilment of banking needs.

This chapter discusses banking generally; the next focuses on credit cards in particular. CRM activities should also take place within a similar framework, and we'll get to that in a little while.

I often hear folks saying that general banking analytics is less mature, sophisticated or value additive than asset analytics (particularly credit cards). Hand on heart, I have to agree the assessment is usually true. But why?

With asset products, many organisations have a risk management function to deliver analytics—for acquisition and behavioural scoring, continuous performance monitoring, credit extension, and collections.

Business analytics is usually developed as a counterpoint, to offer a slightly (not radically) different perspective—usually for credit cards. Working in partnership, the two analytical approaches deliver a level of risk optimisation (a balance between risk and return) not otherwise attainable.

The interaction of these different analytical perspectives has fuelled massive growth in analytics for asset products. Not just in credit/risk but also in performance evaluation, understanding customer behaviour, measuring marketing effectiveness, and predicting future behaviours.

But there is no analogue within more generalised and traditional retail banking (excluding credit cards), even with a substantial asset product footprint (like personal loans and mortgages). Consequently, the rationale for analytics is purely around finding opportunities to add value to existing practices and approaches. In this chapter we'll identify some areas where you can find those opportunities.

Let's start with an overview of cross-selling.

Cross-selling Framework

There are usually a few clearly identifiable and distinct customer bases within any retail bank. Such groups are characterised by: (a) a large number of customers who are unique to each base; and (b) overlap customers, who hold products in more than one base.

For simplicity's sake, let's assume there are three bases:

- Credit Cards: generic, co-brands, etc.

- Lending: mortgage, personal loans, hire-purchase, etc.

- Banking: the umbrella proposition (e.g. Standard, Premium) and the products (checking, investments, stock trading, debit card, and so on).

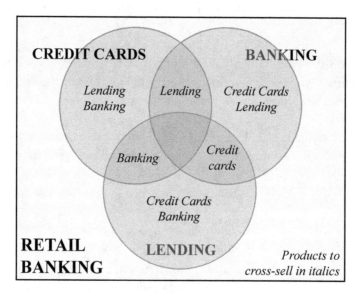

Figure 13.1 The Retail Banking Customer Universe

Figure 13.1 shows how the different bases combine to form the total retail banking customer universe. Cross-sell opportunities are shown in italics.

Note: It can be insightful to populate a similar framework with customer volumes, to demonstrate how major segments overlap, and provide a structure for assigning broad cross-sell goals and aspirations.

From Credit Cards to...

Card-only customers can be cross-sold lending and/or mainstream banking services. These rich opportunities are discussed in the next chapter.

From Lending to...

Cross-selling lending-only customers into other bases is hard work. Data that might be used to build targeting analytics is limited to the application details and some repayment history. Not much that we can build on.

There's also no real brand strength, since products tend to be commoditised and selected on the basis of price, convenience, or the leverage of a third-party relationship.

From Banking to...

Mortgage and personal loan cross-selling is usually a highly time-constrained opportunity. As such, it's rare to see effective predictive modelling techniques.

Cross-selling credit cards should be a high priority; they represent a source of rich data that can enhance our understanding of customer behaviour and potential product needs. It can be challenging to unlock the value; we'll get to that in a moment.

Analytical Resources Required

We are concerned here with general banking (excluding credit cards).

The most significant analytical opportunities are in working the customer base to cross-sell and up-sell the numerous banking products—it's not just credit cards and lending. There are two different types of effort required.

Production Resources

These are the analysts building data marts, or pulling lists for marketing campaigns, or working search engine optimisation, or delivering basic management information. Just how many you need will depend on a variety of factors, including the technical environment, scale of marketing activities, major product groups, distribution model, and so on.

Advanced Analytics Resources

It's much easier to identify the support required for advanced analytics, primarily predictive modelling. The *minimum* support level is shown in figure 13.2.

To be clear, these analysts work exclusively on advanced analytics... *NOT* generating customer lists, management information and reporting, or anything else that production resources work on... and *NOT* working on credit card projects.

SMALL *(<US$250 million revenue):* 1 FTE

MEDIUM *(<US$500 million revenue):* 2 FTE

LARGE *(≥US$500 million revenue):* 3 FTE

+ one per additional $250 million

Figure 13.2 Wealth Management Advanced Analytics Resources

Remember, this is the minimum standard. If you want to gain a significant competitive advantage or accelerate change, then it needs to be more.

The real value of these analysts is in deepening customer relationship. But first, we have to acquire those customers and get them on-board.

Engagement Phase

The engagement phase starts immediately following acquisition of a new customer. It represents the initial stages of their banking relationship, the first transactions and interactions. During this phase we are attempting to establish beneficial customer behaviours—at its most simple, ensuring the account is fully funded and servicing is initiated. We are trying to shape customer behaviour, and it's far more easily done early rather than later.

We'll deal with approaches when we discuss CRM and offers-in-context in later chapters.

Tracking of new accounts is needed as they progress through early engagement. As discussed in the previous chapter on acquisition, borrow from the Risk Management playbook and always evaluate early account performance using the months-on-book approach.

As a minimum, generate separate tracking reports for each month of acquisition. Building out from this minimum, consider other drill-down dimensions such as channels, campaigns, lead-acquisition product, proposition, and branch/region. With so much to consider, think about what makes sense for your business.

Which account metrics should you be tracking? Average balance and customer value as a minimum, but consider additional metrics like opt-out rate, closed accounts, investments cross-sell penetration, etc. We're looking for confirmation that accounts are performing as expected, and monitoring for warning signals of trouble ahead.

You've around six months to shape some behaviours, but tracking new account performance can take longer.

How Long is the Engagement Phase?

The length of this engagement period can vary hugely. Customers with relatively simple banking needs and a single primary banking relationship will swiftly establish their long-term behaviour pattern with you. They'll transfer balances, move continuous authorisations, direct debits, and standing orders. Even for a relatively simple account, it can be an arduous and time-consuming process—there are plenty of hurdles for customers changing their primary banking relationship.

More affluent customers typically have more complicated banking arrangements. These need more time; unravelling positions before transferring to your bank. Other considerations include:

-   Are you becoming the primary relationship or a secondary player? As the primary, it takes longer to establish the new account.

- Have you set a specific performance hurdle the customer needs to achieve to unlock a reward or bonus rate? This will speed up basic setup (say, moving in balances to trigger a bonus rate).

- Customer residence overseas always introduces additional complexity and time. And heaven help you if the setup requires wet signatures.

Best case, engagement is three months and thereafter the longer-term transactions and behaviours are reasonably stable. Worst case, the engagement period is up to 16 months—this for offshore customers, with multiple positions needing to be unwound (TDs, structured notes, etc) before transfer.

Development Phase

Engagement should set customers on a good trajectory, with some early successes in deepening relationships. Development seeks to ensure that emerging customer needs are met and that relationships are further deepened. The most obvious expression of these goals is through cross-sell, up-sell and new funds acquisition.

The Cross-sell Analytics Approach

We're seeking to build targeting models that will predict the likelihood of a customer responding to a new product offer. Back in Chapter 7, "Predictive Analytics Toolbox", we considered two approaches:

- Response models. We randomly make a product offer to customers, then compare those that took-up the offer with those that didn't. Advantage: highly predictive. Disadvantages: time-consuming, expensive, and requires a large number of customers.

- Look-alike/propensity models. Compare customers who currently have the product with those that don't. Advantages: fast, cheap and straightforward. Disadvantages: less predictive than response models, sometimes considerably so.

Let's be pragmatic here. We're trying to improve the effectiveness of sales and marketing, not making a business-critical interest rate hedge. Use the look-alike approach unless you have the luxury of time and budget.

Cross-selling Credit Cards

In some markets, cross selling a credit card to a retail customer is a slam-dunk, in others it's more of a challenge. Fierce credit card competition can drive high value propositions, cut-throat interest rates and highly attractive acquisition offers and premiums; it can be difficult to stand out. But credit card take-up by existing customers increases loyalty, improves brand perception, and (importantly) provides a rich source of data that can improve understanding of customer needs and wants.

It's straightforward to build a cross-sell model using retail customer transactions, behaviours, and demographics. Unfortunately, in a cut-throat market, this delivers a x3, x4 or x5 improvement on an initially low response rate—the economics still may not stack-up. An alternative approach is to use analytics to build a tailored proposition for your base.

You probably know a lot about the target customers: their holdings with you; their demographics; possibly their total affluence or potential. You might have checking/saving account activity including ATM withdrawals, standing orders, and spend in different categories and locations (including overseas). And you also have the existing overlap customers (with a banking relationship and a credit card) which will give further insights.

Data mine to find lifestyle patterns of behaviour. Golf Card? Spa Card? Family Card? Maybe there's an opportunity for travel-related benefits—airline lounge access or free travel insurance? What about a credit card promise: "no fees or charges... ever" (annual fee, late and over-limit, maybe even cash handling)? Work the existing overlap base to scope any expense and/or foregone revenue implications.

Cross-selling Insurance

All insurance cross-selling can benefit from targeting analytics. The targeting models are uncomplicated to build and generate good results.

Often, selling a single low cost, high perceived value insurance product can unlock future possibilities—it's like a big flag saying the customer is relatively risk averse and/or favourable towards insurance.

Data availability can be an issue, particularly identifying specific products. Work might be needed.

There is always a danger with higher ticket insurances that the lust for revenue impedes common sense. If, even after targeting, a campaign is delivering a low response rate, then *don't make the offer*. If you really must make it, don't use a high impact channel... you'll risk upsetting a bunch of customers. We'll get into this theme in more detail when we discuss CRM.

Cross-selling Investments

Rather than individual targeting models for investment products (e.g. equities, unit trusts etc), consider building a unified investments model initially, particularly if your struggling to find volumes for modelling individual products.

Don't include products such as margin finance or currency linked deposits; customer behaviours can be very different than mainstream investors.

If volumes are large enough, develop product specific approaches.

Other Cross-selling

The analytical approach is the same as other products: build a look-alike model if there is suitable volume.

Any product with a low number of customers will likely be (a) difficult to model, resulting in low response rates; and (b) of limited impact to the business (unless there's a very good reason why there was a low volume of customers in the first place).

Upsell and New Fund Acquisition

Cross-selling effort recognises customer need, fulfils it with specific products, and as a consequence deepens the relationship. Upselling and new fund acquisition consolidates that relationship and builds value for both the customer and the bank.

The primary upselling opportunity upgrades customers to higher propositions, e.g. Standard to Gold, or Gold to Premium.

Models to target customers for such upgrades can be problematic. The key issues are not easy to predict: (a) whether the customer has sufficient off-us funds to qualify; and (b) are they prepared to commit them? New fund acquisition faces similar issues.

This is where customer potential measures (discussed in Chapter 10, "Customer Metrics") are extremely useful. Target with upscale propositions and new fund promotions to those with a clear disparity between current holdings and expected affluence.

Operational Considerations

Additional banking analytics are discussed in Chapter 15, "Lifecycle Analytics: Retention".

There are also analytical needs that fall outside the lifecycle framework, particularly relating to operations, servicing, and customer experience. For example:

- ATM replenishment planning—an old-school Operational Research network optimisation problem, married to predictions of usage.

- Sentiment analysis has been around for a while and has gained new momentum with its application via social media. It's like having an instant "pulse check" on brand strength, service quality, and campaign recognition.

- Call tree load balancing and skills-based routing. Optimising the distribution of calls to available operators; and simplifying customer experience.

- Application (and website) navigation studies. Not high-end analytics, but potentially very high impact. Done well, it requires mastery of experimental design (see Chapter 11 for the basic concepts).

With the exception of the latter, these are relatively sporadic and lower-value analytical opportunities. A few of higher profile are shown below—not an exhaustive list, but sufficient to demonstrate some of the possibilities.

Fund Flows

If you've got large outflows, the concern is often "Where did the money go?". The relatively simple way to do this is to view the customer account as a black box: stuff goes in, stuff comes out, ending with a net positive or negative impact. If this analysis hasn't been attempted before, you will probably discover a host of data issues as you try to map transaction codes to fund sources and destinations.

Sometimes, the real question being asked is something like "Can the reduction in deposit volumes be explained by an increase in investments?". A seemingly innocuous and straightforward question, but beware the analytical quicksand here. Attribution of movements can be highly complex; identifying causation even more so.

Punchline: Resolving data issues is a valuable exercise. Understanding fund-flows is an interesting intellectual activity. But if you have an issue with fund attrition, don't be side-tracked by fund flows; manage the attrition directly (see Chapter 15).

Sales Incentives

These are sometimes frustrating to support. Whilst the analytic requirement is light, there are people challenges.

Typically, there will be a cut-off date by which time sales staff are required to have logged all their sales. These are then processed to derive individual, team, branch and maybe even sales region goals (it depends on the design of the incentive scheme).

This is real money, but people make mistakes. They might forget a sale, or they don't have time to enter it before the deadline, or they're out of the office/on vacation/sick, or they were kidnapped, or they were delayed by a majestic herd of wildebeest sweeping across the expressway to the office (my apologies to Basil Fawlty). The list of excuses is seemingly inexhaustible. And they'll all be used at some point, in an attempt to force a rerun of the commission calculations... because a single sale can make or break goal achievement, potentially for many people.

To make it work, have clear rules-of-engagement and rigid deadlines. Do not expect a junior analyst to disappoint their client by refusing to update an analysis. They can't, so don't make them. All requests for extension need to be made to the analytics Head of Department and decided in consultation with the Head of Sales (or equivalent). The seniority of sign-off will (hopefully) ensure that requests are made on an exceptional basis.

Branch Optimisation

What is the right number of branches? Which branches are under/over performing? What is the right level of staffing in each branch?

The migration of customer transactions, interactions and servicing to online and remote channels has placed the traditional branch-based model under the spot-light... and in the crosshairs. Branches are expensive.

Critical to any evaluation of network performance are:

-   Measures of branch performance. Customer volumes; customer value; branch characteristics (size, number of tellers), staffing (number, experience and seniority. There are many potential metrics and ratios; start with something like customer value per square foot—it's a metric that can be compared across the network.

-   Comparative performance may not be sufficient; you might also need to consider branch performance relative to the potential. That requires:

    a) A definition of each branch catchment. Gravity modelling; geographical accessibility; travel times; etc. Analytically straightforward.

    b) A measure of branch potential. Residential and business employee numbers and affluence within each catchment. This is heavily dependent on data availability. You may need to use high level estimates; or even counting people on the street.

Branch re-engineering is a hot topic. It's not just about optimising the right branches in the right locations. It's also about further digitising interactions, reskilling staff and expanding the purpose and function of the branch. All this is built upon a foundation of really understanding current performance.

HR Analytics

This is gaining traction: the application of analytics to improve aspects of workforce performance, using the data you hold on those employees.

Maybe it's pre-screening new applicants for a better organisational fit, identifying employee attrition trends, or spotting potential leadership issues.

A lack of accessible data will probably stymy you—it's unstructured, or there are restrictive interpretations of data (and employee) protection requirements, or it's just not captured.

Start with something relatively achievable, like a profiling questionnaire for potential new employees... think Myers-Briggs rather than Clarice Starling. At the same time, begin the redesign of documentation and processes to facilitated future analysis.

A Note of Caution

The analytical opportunities covered here are not a definitive list, nor can they be. The canvas is too broad.

With multiple products and customer segments, all manner of behaviours and situations can be investigated, data-mined, modelled, and predicted. Retail banking is a vibrant, exciting and hugely satisfying area to work in... and (done well) analytics can contribute *massively* to business success.

But getting an analytical foothold can be difficult. Persevere. Success requires senior management focus, an organisation wide commitment to change, and relentless engagement between analytics, business and distribution owners.

And to further frustrate analytical ambitions, there will likely be data issues to overcome:

- Gaps, inconsistencies, and discontinuities in your internal data;

- A lack of documentation about how to interpret what you do have; and,

- Huge black holes from third-party suppliers of mutual funds, stock trading, insurance, and other products.

Work through the issues and realise the benefits. You will not be disappointed.

CHAPTER 14

Lifecycle Analytics: Credit Cards

The application of analytics to credit cards is relatively mature and well established, primarily driven by (a) risk management sophistication, and (b) the US monoline card issuers who emerged during the late '80s and fuelled massive card and receivables growth during the '90s and beyond.

That was then, and this is now. The world is changing, and despite continued strong sales volume growth, the outlook is far less rosy for the associations and the issuers than it was twenty, ten or even five years ago. Consider:

- New payment mechanisms and platforms are eroding card payment share;

- Regulators are waking up to less customer-friendly industry practices (including high interchange, rigged payment hierarchies, and exploitational line increases);

- The lending landscape is changing. Choices for short- and long-term credit are proliferating and instantly available at competitive rates (or even interest- and fee-free); and,

- The whole idea of carrying plastic is increasingly archaic and anachronistic, not just to millennials. The relevance of cards might fade away.

The associations and card issuers are not sleepwalking to extinction. They are trying to adapt and maintain their relevance, but the jury is out on how successful those efforts will ultimately prove to be.

In the meantime, "there's life in the old dog yet" and legacy card businesses and customers continue to present business and analytical opportunities. And many of the examples shown here apply across multiple products and approaches, not just cards.

Engagement Phase

The length of the engagement phase should reflect the time it takes for a new account to reach *normal performance*. For credit cards, spend levels build in the first few months, and balances and write-offs typically stabilise around MOB 15 to 24. Your window to influence behaviours is much shorter, you've probably got the first few months, six at most.

We will discuss mechanisms for driving behaviour during the engagement phase as part of CRM and offers-in-context; they can require complex tracking. Early estimation of likely behaviour is useful to help drive these engagement actions—say, understanding whether a cardholder is more likely to be a transactor than a revolver.

There's a time trade-off here. New accounts have the application demographics alone. Over time, you'll build additional intelligence on spending preferences and volumes, overseas transaction patterns, revolving balances and payments. This is all useful for predicting future behaviours.

In early vintage try a simple proxy approach: use your risk application score in reverse to predict likely revolver versus transactor i.e. high approval rate = low risk and low revolve; lower approval rate = higher risk and higher revolve.

Development Phase

By this lifecycle phase, cardholders have settled into long-term behaviours. Our objectives here are to meet product needs and deepen relationships.

We'll deal with the communication implications when we consider CRM in more detail. For now, here's a laundry list of the typical programmes used in cardholder development. I'm focussing here on analytical considerations and potential opportunities and pitfalls.

Balance transfer, where we're paying down debt on an external credit card using the cardholders open-to-buy credit line on our card, with a promotional rate and promotional period. *Credit card check* programs offer similar utility but are often not restricted to paying down an external line. That's more like a "balance transfer to self", where the cardholder ultimately ends up with cash or a deposit to a nominated bank account.

Balance transfer predictive models should be used for the transactor base. They are very effective, the target base is large, response rates to BT offers are low, and scoring can deliver a strong KS (you can probably drop 75% of targets with a tiny impact on response volume).

There's no need for sophisticated targeting to revolvers. They'll take anything and often at any price. We'll revisit this in Chapter 18, "CRM Across the Lifecycle".

For now, take a look at the card segmentation in the appendices, which shows how this approach might work.

Pricing is usually an under-developed discipline within cards groups and often represents an unrealised opportunity. Let's briefly consider five types of pricing here:

- *Acquisition pricing*, i.e. the standard rates (for cash and retail) a new customer receives. Many issuers (at least across Asia) continue to use "one size fits all", rather than using price to better reflect expected risk/return or as part of the card value proposition. The effectiveness of such approaches obviously depends heavily on consumer knowledge/sophistication and price sensitivity.

- *Behavioural pricing*, as a mechanism to adjust standard rates based upon observed behaviours from the customer. This means lowering rates for good customers, increasing them for the bad, and adjusting continuously as the risk profile improves/degrades.

  The best approaches are transparent to customers, e.g. you miss two payments, your rate goes up a bit (as a slap on the wrist and to better reflect my potential risk) until you convince me you're ok.

Finally, three behavioural pricing tenets:

1. You must be fair to the customer. This is not a profit gouging opportunity; it is pricing for risk.

2. You can't do this everywhere; jurisdictions have different regulatory requirements.

3. For the highest risk customers, pricing doesn't have much impact; they'll go bad, whatever the rate.

- *Existing customer promotional pricing (for BT and instalment loans).* This was touched on when discussing acquisition effectiveness evaluation; we'll return to it again later.

For simplicity here: "Don't give away the farm". Use your communications with the customer to build an understanding of their pricing elasticity; initially price high and gradually come down. This take enormous nerve from the business head (particularly when missing a short-term target), but every shred of analytical evidence says once you anchor a customer at a price point, they are difficult to move up. So, for goodness' sake, don't anchor them at the bottom.

> **It's possible to get a blended yield increase of up to 50% over previous pricing approaches**

The business impact of improved yield can be significant and generates considerable incremental value from existing customers.

- *Annual fees.* Here just as a placeholder, because there are other considerations related to the economics of annual fees, waivers and attrition. We'll discuss further in the upcoming chapter on retention.

- *Nuisance charges.* These mostly follow a herd mentality: a competitor increases a charge (e.g. late payment, declined check) and other issuers follow. Do the charges reflect additional operational expenses, additional exposure risk, or some other genuine increase in customer management expense? Probably not. Quantify this for clarity and transparency in internal decision making and in case the regulator comes calling.

Opportunities for applying analytics to pricing are potentially huge, but it takes dedicated analytical expertise.

Pricing impacts are often subtle or gradually evolve. Business goals are usually more short term and desperate circumstances can drive desperate measures, including repricing the whole book upwards. You will need senior analytical leadership to temper such immediate business ambition with analytical common-sense. I've had a few difficult conversations about short-term revenue versus longer-term portfolio health.

Instalment plan, where a transaction or balance converts to an instalment plan within an existing credit line, with a fixed term and fixed monthly payment amount (interest + principal repayment).

Done well, such programs encourage responsible borrowing by cardholders and can unlock incremental value when selectively targeting cardholders with a low likelihood of revolving.

Done badly, instalment plans border on the unscrupulous and/or immoral—charging high upfront arrangement fees and allowing long terms.

That said, some of the most successful campaigns to existing instalment cardholders are *top-up* or *reload* programmes. No need to target; hit everyone at three, two, and one month to full term. Do not compromise on price; you're extremely unlikely to increase the price from the previous rate; keep it the same as initially booked. If you must decrease, use champion/challenger (the existing price versus the new, lower price) over the medium term (say, six months) to assess performance.

Instalment programmes can present a problem for your receivables structure. The more instalments you book, the higher the run-off of core interest bearing receivables, e.g. if everything is on a 20-month tenure, then every month you lose 5% of the instalment receivables. You can outrun it for a while, as new instalment bookings obscure the underlying trend; but it will catch up with you and probably need significant top-up/reload activities, particularly if the instalments have replaced some revolving receivables.

Finally, there may be a further unforeseen problem with significant instalment volumes: you affect the spend behaviours because the open-to-buy line space is being squeezed. This particularly hurts if you've been successful in selling instalments to your high transactors. Carefully consider your strategy for such customers before jumping on the instalment treadmill.

If you use instalment programmes, proactively analyse the portfolio structure and turn-over to forecast likely future implications.

Personal Instalment Loan (PIL) cross-sell to cardholders. Typically, the business owner of the card business will be fiercely protective of his customers and their credit lines. But sometimes it just makes sense to offer a PIL rather than a card line extension, say if:

- the customer never revolves;

- you want to offer a lower price without compromising the positioning of the card pricing;

- you are offering a *true* debt consolidation product; or

- the customer requests it.

If you perform line extensions each month, then volumes might be small, and analytical possibilities limited. If line extensions are done periodically, then there are more opportunities for analytics. Either way, a head-to-head test of line extension versus PIL is a good place to start. Which delivers the best longer-term performance? The answer is far from straightforward and requires extensive testing and tracking.

Spend stimulation programmes can serve several purposes. Straight-out spend stim can reward customers, promote particular merchants, and/or reinforce the value proposition of the card (or issuer bank or association). The aim is simple: to inspire the cardholders to spend (on an activity, with a merchant, or within a category).

The programmes can also be used tactically, as part of reactivation efforts. For example, where a cardholder has gone quiet for a while, or has reduced spend (often a precursor of long-term inactivity or account closure). But often, spend stimulation programs are bigger and bolder, broadly targeted and supported with significant above-the-line marketing.

Building revolving balances can be an ambition of these programmes, and balance stickiness is baked into the financial assumptions behind the programme—occasionally using wildly ambitious targets.

There's not much we can add analytically to these programmes, other than ensuring appropriate tracking is in place for a fair and honest interpretation of results. Sometimes establishing appropriate control groups is a challenge, a function of either (a) the use of above-the-line media to publicise the offer; and/or (b) word-of-mouth gets to the control groups anyway (or they ring to complain their friend got it, and they didn't). It's easier to establish controls when dealing with a more focused, smaller volume and targeted programmes.

Tracking should show that spend increases; but activity will usually revert to the previous pattern. Reversion might take as long as three months for a longer duration (say, one month) promotion.

One final word of caution. Some spend stimulation programmes require monetary adjustments to a customer account, e.g. "Spend $100 and we'll credit you $4". If this involves the analytics function (to identify the customers, or the adjustment amounts) then involvement in the campaign design is necessary, to make sure that the campaign objectives are practical and realisable.

Cash advance fee waivers offer a promotional period of zero or reduced transaction charge for ATM cash advances. The underlying rationale is: (a) change customer behaviour to use cash advances in future (with a fee); and/or, (b) some cash advance will convert to a revolving balance.

It's critical that performance is measured, since such campaigns usually lose money. There is a small uptick in cash advances, but it quickly returns to pre-promotional levels (just like spend stimulation) and has almost no impact on revolve—both when compared with a control. Plus, existing cash advance users get a free ride for the duration of the campaign. Use control groups for these promotions to measure true lift impacts.

Cash advances can signal a high risk, and the whole charging structure reflects this: a high handling fee, zero interest free days and often a higher interest rate payable on balances. There's a "chicken and egg" thing going on here, and the transactions might be high risk because the significant cost associated with them drives away the low-risk customer usage.

Supplementary card promotion economics should be reviewed occasionally. There is usually diminishing marginal returns. The first supp is profitable, the second less so, anything subsequent is frequently underwater. Analytically determine the best point to cease promoting additional cards.

Card conversions, or upgrades, are most successful when offered with an increased credit line (particularly in jurisdictions where the customer needs to accept any additional line). Conversions increase spend and revolve if the new card carries prestige (and therefore the customer wants to show it off). Again, occasionally analyse the economics.

Affinity and co-brand card businesses are often predicated on "showing off the card", because the customer is proud (and sometimes preening). The Ferrari Card, "Don't Mess with Texas" (one of few successful geographical affinities), and top tier universities all spring to mind.

The economics of these cards can be perilous since payments to partner organisations, and rewards to customers can destroy profitability. The overhead of supporting smaller customer bases can also become onerous.

Make all payments to partners contingent upon profitability; admittedly a tough sell to powerful brands with attractive customer bases.

Track ongoing performance using Customer Value. There are pluses and minuses to incorporating the card reward/rebate dynamics into the CV calculation... and too much detail to consider here.

Continuous Authorisations

Regular payments of any type increase customer stickiness. Continuous Authorisations are particularly effective—they show long-term customer commitment to using the card, plus become additional hurdles to card cancellation.

Some issuers have built platforms to allow automatic utility payments on cards (similar to standing instructions) specifically to exploit this stickiness.

Insurance cross-sell has been a mainstay of credit card revenue diversification and enhancement for decades, although the fallout from the payment protection insurance (PPI) mis-selling scandal in the UK has dampened enthusiasm for some products.

Targeting analytics work well, the models are uncomplicated to build, and generate good results.

My previous observations on insurance cross-sell to general banking customers also hold true here. Selling a single low cost, high perceived value insurance product may unlock future higher value possibilities. The product palette is typically smaller than for wealth management: credit protection, redundancy protection, travel, and basic health (e.g. hospital cash).

Cross-selling banking proposition (Premium, Gold, Standard, etc) might be geographically constrained. For example, card issuance is countrywide, whilst the branch footprint is more regional—it's particularly an issue in the USA. Digital is undoubtedly removing such constraints, but the brand awareness and trust of regional banks still holds much appeal.

Where there are no geographical constraints, the proposition cross-sell should always appear in any catalogue of card actions. You might build an out-and-out response model (but that's expensive), or you could try a look-alike approach using the overlap population with an existing banking relationship and a credit card. Standard stuff and effective.

Remember though, that often the customer came for the card proposition and that's all they want.

Risk and Operational Considerations

There are a few other applications of analytics that don't fit within the lifecycle framework.

Credit line increases become less effective at higher levels. A line increase from $2,000 to $2,500 is significantly better utilised (percentage wise) than an increase from $20,000 to $25,000. If your Risk Management function worries about contingent liability, then give up the high-end line increases in favour of lots of smaller ones.

Utilisation stalling can occur in dramatic fashion. In the US, there can be a clear step change in utilisation rates above and below $10,000, almost as though customers viewed this as a comfort ceiling. In the UK it was £10,000. Check it out for your portfolio.

Dunning letters will always benefit from a readability review. Over 30 years ago, my great friend Bob Beattie undertook a text analysis on collection letters for a major UK catalogue retailer and concluded:

- The early-stage delinquency letters started with a reading age of 13 years. Various studies have put the average reading age in the UK somewhere between 9 and 12 years old.

- As the severity of the delinquency increased, the reading age required to understand the letters also increased. At the end of the cycle, you needed a college/university degree to understand the message.

Improving readability inevitably improves collections effectiveness and yet remains an under exploited area.

That original analysis was done by hand: counting word lengths, the number of words per sentence, negative and passive verbs, etc. These days it's much easier; Microsoft Word even has readability measures included. Use them to assess your collections letters.

Collections scoring predicts the probability of delinquent customers' repaying. This can then prioritise collection calling to those in the middle score range: don't waste effort on those who are likely to repay anyway, or those who are unlikely to repay. Do the evaluations to confirm this.

Rewards points are often one of the largest expense lines for a card business, and there are two significant areas where analytics can add value. The first is assessing the level of provisioning. This was briefly touched upon during our earlier customer value discussion (in Chapter 10).

Data on redemptions is often unavailable or incomplete. Work is usually required to identify and prepare sources for analysis.

If the rewards programme is close ended (i.e. points have a fixed lifetime) then use previous experience for provisioning. But for open-ended or "evergreen" programmes (where points never expire) establishing the correct level of provisioning is trickier. Using open accounts will low-ball the true redemption rate and result in under provisioning. There's only one group you can use for estimation: cardholders who have previously closed their accounts; look at their lifetime earn and burn.

Once you've completed the analysis, there is normally a significant level of additional provisioning costs for open-ended versus closed-end programmes.

Another opportunity for rewards analytics is to identify the high value reward redeemers (usually travel related rewards, so you could also build an outright *travel junkie* score). Use this for burn booster programmes to change behaviour, e.g. deeply discounted points for specific non-travel redemption items, creating a high customer perceived value, but at a cost below the travel reward alternatives.

I've seen dramatically different levels of expertise in rewards management across different credit card operations. Active management and high expertise will always deliver *substantial and sustainable* cost savings.

Market Information Leverage

I want to discuss one last item of card analytics... but it's not easily exploited. You might not be large enough to generate robust data, or you might face regulatory hurdles.

I'm talking about the use of credit card spending data for a couple of specific applications. Both need scale.

Assessment of the Macro-economic Environment

Once your credit card spend volume gets north of 20% market share, you have the power to predict the overall health of the economy. Traditionally card spend correlates with overall levels of retail spend, which correlates with consumer confidence, GDP growth and general macro-economic health.

A higher market share delivers greater visibility of the macro situation. This data is more immediate than any government or association sources; more reliable than market research or sentiment analysis. And where there is an information advantage, there is commercial value.

It's fairly straightforward analytics. You need to understand your cardholder demographic profile versus the market and use weightings to normalise. This is a good example of leveraging traditional market research in combination with big data analytics.

I've not done an empirical assessment, but I think it highly likely that:

- As the proportion of non-card spend rises, macro-economic predictiveness falls; but should be *directionally* correct up to a point.

- Players with a card spend share of less than 20% can still work this, but you need a deep understanding of your demographics versus the market, and there may be geographical constraints (where your representation is weakest).

I first played with this approach back in the 90s. I was working with a double-digit market share of card spend, knew my demographic profile versus market, but had limited historical data so couldn't effectively validate results. Subsequently, I've had more success.

Retail Competition Analysis

This is astonishing easy, and you can make it work with less than 20% spend share, particularly in market sectors where you have relative strength. You can assess the performance of any retail business by looking at the sales data from your cardholders.

Use this market intelligence for:

- Assessing individual store or chain performance (a) in isolation; or (b) in comparison with their competition.

- Monitoring the health of a specific merchant category using anonymised data and not exposing the performance of an individual retailer.

- Providing early warning alerts to Risk Management about an individual category or retailer performance. This might better inform your commercial/SME credit operations.

You might even use this information to convince upmarket retailers to provide exclusive store offers or discount nights to cardholders. And if there's no enthusiasm from the market leader, talk to the market #2.

Implementation Considerations

Higher levels of non-card spend are increasingly a function of market payment sophistication. Ten years ago, it was the opposite and high non-card spending showed market immaturity.

Fintech innovations are driving the expansion of POS payment options in most markets. This will impact the accuracy of these types of analysis.

Leverage also depends on regulations (particularly data protection), contract wording (for cardholders and merchants) and a bunch of other local sensitivities.

All I'm doing here is planting analytical ideas; I'm not commenting on the viability for specific markets or businesses.

CHAPTER 15

Lifecycle Analytics: Retention

Some level of customer attrition is inevitable. Service failures happen, competitors will compete, and customers will leave. But some attrition is avoidable and preventable, and the application of analytics can certainly help in retention efforts.

It seems like a no-brainer: build a model to predict the customers most likely to attrite and get to them with an offer to make them stay.

As usual with these kinds of things, it's not so simple. Don't get me wrong, the models themselves are straightforward to build, highly predictive and extremely robust. But that predictive mechanism exists within a wider business context, which includes:

- All business decisions leading to where the customer might attrite.

    Maybe the acquisition offer is driving the wrong behaviour. Maybe you've over-contacted the customer and they want peace and quiet. Maybe you've changed their branch/RM/tier status adversely. Some of these decisions are probably easier to recover from than others.

- The potential business response. Many possible treatments or approaches might be attempted to reverse the loss of each customer.

    Should you proactively try to stop them? Or wait until the attrition is obvious? Or just let them go? What offers should you make and over what channels?

So, let's take this a step at a time.

Problem Definition

First, let's be clear about how to define the problem. We can define customer attrition in two ways:

Silent. When a customer pays down a credit facility or clears all balances or ceases to transact. The account stays open, but all that remains is an empty (or near empty) shell.

Overt. When the account is closed. Attrition is clear and unambiguous.

From a business reporting perspective, it is tempting to report the overt number alone. The assumption is that silent attritors haven't actually gone and they will/can be reactivated. That's a big (and probably unrealistic) assumption and, as a general rule, the longer the period of inactivity, the more difficult to reactivate the customer.

A subset of (and precursor to) silent attrition is *balance attrition*—a significant reduction in customer balances (the situation is similar for assets and liabilities). The reduction might be sudden or gradual, but the result is the same: a low residual balance in the account.

There's an implied timeline: balance attrition comes before silent attrition as the customer clears out each account; and then the customer may remain as a silent attritor before final overt attrition. It doesn't have to be that way; the customer could just clear out and leave in one visit to a branch (or website if you allow online account closure).

Given these behaviours, it's no surprise attrition predictive models include variables like "time since active" and "decline in balance over the last two months".

Often, attempts are made to use analytics as a "quick fix" for an attrition issue. But building a predictive model and then targeting probable attritors is usually the wrong approach and destined for failure.

Whenever considering attrition, the first steps should always be to consider root causes.

Attrition Root Causes

Don't simply use analytics to identify potential attritors and attempt to save them; you might be papering over fundamental problems. Use analytics to determine root causes so that they can be addressed.

Sometimes, causes are obvious (or at least discoverable): customer service failures, long wait times for call handling, poor digital functionality, etc. These are also relatively easy to fix. But sometimes, the cause can be harder to identify.

Look at acquisition practices to ensure these are not driving an element of attrition. If you're offering teaser rates (often used for mortgages and credit cards), then ensure you have a plan for managing customers before they come off that rate. Same thing for bonus deposit rates. In fact, you must manage any time-constrained offer in a similar way. Think about the customer journey, plan choices and manage the customer transition to the post-offer state. Make that planning part of the campaign design, considered up front before you launch. *Don't leave it until the last minute or treat it as an afterthought.*

Plan and implement early engagement and development actions targeting under-utilised customers. Keep trying to deepen relationships—more products, higher balances, and greater transaction volumes are all drivers of increased customer stickiness.

Over-contact can be an issue, so look at the data. Are attritors being contacted significantly more than similar non-attriting customers? Drowning customers in irrelevant, unwanted offers is never productive. Conversely, not contacting the customer enough can also lead to customer disillusionment, disengagement and departure.

Treating root causes is a laudable goal and will certainly improve business performance over the medium and longer term. But it doesn't help much with the "right here, right now" reality when customers are walking out the door.

What else can be done to quell the tide? And when should you intervene?

Customer Reengagement

Once a customer becomes inactive, the clock is ticking. The longer they remain inactive, the less likely they are to reengage. For most products, the chances of reengagement after six months of inactivity are only a handful of percentage points, and it can be even less.

Figure 15.1 demonstrates the likelihood of customer reengagement. We made no offer to the customers here. We're just measuring self-reengagement, where the customer spontaneously becomes active again with no (known) external influence.

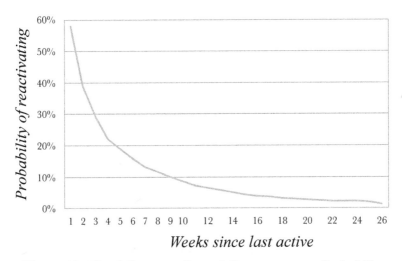

Figure 15.1 Dual Currency Deposit Reengagement Probability

In this example, a customer who's inactive for one week is less than 60% likely to reactivate. After 9 weeks, it's 10%, and 26 weeks is less than 1%. This is *extreme* product disengagement.

At the product level, disengagement and reengagement is an inevitable part of the typical product usage cycle. For a relationship with multiple products, single product events are usually not significant attrition indicators; but where balances and/or activity decline across multiple products, there could be a relationship threat.

So, how do you identify a behaviour that is atypical and most likely a precursor for attrition? Should you attempt to intervene? If so, when?

Proactive Approaches

One approach is to consider an intervention when you observe a customer becoming inactive. In the early stages of inactivity, you might adopt a "wait and see" approach, just in case a customer re-engages. For a longer period of inactivity, you may not want to wait; you could give them a nudge in the right direction to help them become active again.

Targeted Re-engagement

Making approaches to inactive customers is fairly typical, but there is a challenge with this approach, as shown in Figure 15.2 below.

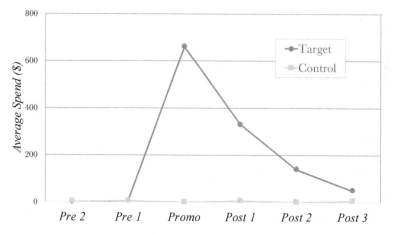

Figure 15.2 Promotional Spending Over Time

This campaign targeted a spend promotion to six-month inactive credit card customers. As the graph shows, post-promotion activity quickly drops back to previous levels.

It is extremely difficult to change a long-established behaviour. But, just like self-reengagement, the probability of sustained improvements is higher if you can get to a customer quickly once they initially become inactive.

It would be even better to identify a customer before they become inactive. Here's a small selection of examples targeting activities that are precursors to inactivity. And if you're making the effort to identify and target them, then make sure you are also trying to build incremental balances or activity, not just save them.

Credit cards:

- Historical revolver; sudden paydown of 25% of balance
- Historical revolver; two consecutive months of balance decline > 10%
- Transactor; spend decline of 10% (or goes to zero, or declines by one standard deviation, or something else)

Retail banking:

- Large outflow: more than US$20k or > 30% of total balances
- Two consecutive months of total balance decline, each > 15%
- Three consecutive months of total balance decline, each > 10%

Larger amounts over shorter periods can be more predictive of problems ahead than smaller amounts over a longer time. Adjust your targeting (amounts, volumes, time, and communication channel) and offers (particularly pricing) to reflect learning.

Whatever the approach, the assumption and ambition are simple. If we can stop the reduction in balances and/or activity, then we can go some way to preventing attrition.

Modelled Approaches

Model targeted attrition prediction is another popular proactive approach. This is the entry-point for most organisations when applying analytics to attrition. Later, as an organisation gathers results and understanding evolves, analytics are applied to reengagement and reactive approaches. A sustainable strategy normally emerges after much trial and error.

But those first steps are the same: build a look-alike model to predict attrition and then target the top X% with a retention offer.

And that's when a fundamental problem should become apparent: *it's really hard to make the economics work*. Mind you, not every organisation will spot this—it's a function of analytical sophistication and engagement. You need to commit to test/control for validating targeting effectiveness and post-campaign performance analysis (for at least a few months).

Here's a simple example highlighting the economic challenges:

- Let's say we target 100 attritors. Assume our predictive model is so good we are 100% accurate; all our targets are about to attrite.

- We make each of them a simple offer: spend an additional $100 in a month and receive a $10 reward. They all accept the offer.

- Assume we already make $10 per month on each retained customer. So, as long as the customers stay for more than a month, we're ahead i.e. we're profit positive for the campaign and have retained the customers for at least the short term. Everything after this is more upside... hurray.

But some assumptions here are unreal. So, let's add just a little real-worldliness:

- 100% predictive accuracy would be awesome. 30% is an excellent real-life expectation. Now, of the 100 customers targeted, only 30 were about to attrite and 70 would have stayed.

- Not everyone who would have attrited will take up the offer. We'll assume it's 50:50, so in this example, 15 customers accept the offer and 15 don't.

- Inevitably, a high proportion of those who weren't going to attrite will also take up the offer. Let's say 75%, so 53 customers.

These three factors have a dramatic impact on payback and performance:

- There's a $680 cost in rewards (15 + 53 customers, each at $10).

- We saved 15 customers. If they deliver $10 per month in revenue, they need to stay with us for four and a half months for us to hit break even.

We're also still dealing with other fairly benign assumptions here. After all, how is a retained customer supposed to deliver $10 per month in revenue? Maybe it's a card customer going from inactive to transacting $1,000 a month and we pocket the interchange. Or maybe it's a retail customer who brought in $6,000 at 2% spread for one month. My point is not that it's impossible to make approaches like this work, just that it's hard.

Someone may well trot out the argument that saving 15 customers for $680 is only $45 per customer, which is a lot cheaper than new acquisition. This thinking is deeply flawed. A longer-term analytical perspective will *always* show these saved customers (when considered on average) are of relatively low value and differ greatly from an average newly acquired customer. Another example of the importance of post-campaign evaluation.

You could try to make a save without offering an incentive. Sometimes, just reaching out and letting the inactive customer know you're there is enough. That might even work using no targeting analytics—but you do still have to perform a robust evaluation *and have a control group*.

Deposit Attrition and Repricing
It's common to experience deposit attrition, usually in the face of competitor aggression on rates.

When confronted with this situation, the dilemma is the same: how to offer a better rate to retain balances without destroying the existing revenues? It's not as though you can immediately reprice the whole book to retain the 1% of balances (or whatever the number is) you're losing each month. But, can you use analytics to target those balances most likely to attrite?

We can frame the solution in the same way as the model targeted approach, and the issues are similar. Consider the moving parts:

- Predictive power. How well can we predict a specific deposit to attrite? It's a difficult predictive task. 20% accuracy would be excellent.

- Take-up rate. Here, it's always 100% since we're repricing everyone in our model targeted segment.

- Offer cost. This is the haircut we have to take on the net interest margin (NIM). The volume of targeted balances will determine how expensive that might be.

- Success rate i.e. the proportion of balances that remain post reprice. Unsurprisingly, the weaker the offer, the lower the success.

The biggest issue is predictive power. The 20% prediction rate has two major implications:

1. All else being equal, 80% of the repriced deposits were not an immediate attrition risk; but we repriced anyway, giving up spread without an immediate need to do so.

2. The 20% prediction rate is likely gained from targeting 10% of the portfolio (those most likely to attrite). This means we're probably not even making an offer to the vast majority of attritors; our overall impact is therefore relatively small.

The inefficiency of the targeting also means that even a relatively small upward price will negatively impact net interest earnings. Inevitably, businesses need to consider more than NIM and may be compelled to make margin reduction decisions irrespective of any analytical logic.

But if you can't reprice, what are your other options? Things I've seen previously include:

- Launch a new deposit product with operational elements clearly different from the vanilla proposition, e.g. tiered rate. Price the new product more attractively and allow customers to self-select.

- Identify reacquisition opportunities. If a customer has typically used 12-month tenure TDs, then it's possible any balance lost to a competitor is parked on the same tenure. Use an offer-in-context to generate a targeted offer at the most appropriate time, e.g. one month before term.

   If you have relationship managers supporting your more upscale customers, then they're likely already doing something similar, albeit with diary entries or scraps of paper in their desk drawer.

   Looking at the destination of such external transfers can also help in understanding which competitors, products or tenures are hurting you.

- Reactively try to respond to potential deposit attrition. We'll deal with that next.

Reactive Approaches

The biggest issue with proactive approaches is the wastage of applying offers to the false positives (those customers the predictive model wrongly thought would attrite). You get few false positives with reactive approaches since we're reacting to an attrition (or near attrition) event.

You need to detect the event in real-time and respond by opening a dialogue with the customer—in the branch, on the phone, or via a chat session online.

You need a dedicated team to handle the dialogue; and they need to engage the customer, determine context and creatively offer solutions.

Credit Card Balance Retention

The credit card market continues to evolve, embracing new technology, delivery systems and revenue opportunities. But the way an issuer primarily makes money remains the same: revolving balances. Every issuer should fight to keep those balances.

Proactive modelled approaches usually deliver limited success, there's too much wastage. But you should still test to be sure.

Reactive approaches deliver the best sustained solution, obviously within the constraints discussed above. Provide the dedicated retention team with pricing guidance and reward performance based upon the weighted rates granted to the customers they handled.

For the balances you miss with this approach, go to your settlement files and identify where the balances went. Resoliciting after the promo period (make a guess what the competition offered) is an option.

Credit Card Annual Fees

Annual fees are sometimes a point of contention. The waiver decision logic should be transparent and verifiable using analysis. Only waive the fee if the customer has cleared a performance threshold, e.g. customer value or spending. Some cards (airline co-brands in particular) exist almost exclusively to drive spend volumes and survive on the thinnest of margins; fees are essential for profitability; don't waive. Prestige cards: don't waive.

If you have significant levels of discontent with annual fees, consider removing them or reconfiguring the product to survive without them.

Obviously, such decisions should be made in light of the total relationship value; but you must be rigidly consistent with card-only customers. And, most importantly: don't simply "waive to save", you're probably just increasing silent attrition.

Attrition Summary

Attrition can be strongly coupled to business decisions made across the customer lifecycle. Sometimes the attrition implications of those decisions are consciously and knowingly made, but mostly they're not.

Acquisition is often the biggest culprit. Things driving attrition include chasing unrealistic new booking volumes, ill-considered acquisition approaches (including promotional rates, customer premiums/gifts, and sales incentives), and a lack of planning on (a) how to deal with an influx of new customers; and (b) how to manage expiring promotional offers. The most impactful retention activity is to *fix these root causes*.

Retention efforts always need to consider the finely balanced economics of trying to save customers. Reactivation of inactive accounts is difficult to do profitably. Proactive anti-attrition efforts are also tough to make viable.

Profitability is often helped by using the retention effort as an opportunity to build incremental balances (or other business)—this works particularly well for credit card balances, but less so for deposits.

It's worth remembering customers are just like Pavlov's Dogs and making retention offers will inevitably train them to expect similar treatment in the future. So, for assets, if you are moving the customer to a lower price point, don't expect too many opportunities to increase the price later on (and vice versa for liabilities).

As with so many other kinds of business problems, the key to successful retention is a careful mix of analytics and business actions, with an evaluation of effectiveness that incorporates control groups and a long-term performance view.

CHAPTER 16

Offers-in-Context

At their simplest, offers-in-context are merely old-style event triggers, i.e. the recognition of a customer event (maybe a transaction or a key date) and the generation of an offer. But typically, the only real context for an event trigger is the relevance of the offer.

We need to find use cases exploiting the four components of context: relevance, timeliness, location, and channel (first introduced in Chapter 2). The greater the context, the more we can leverage a situation or event to the advantage of both the customer and the business.

Let's consider each aspect of context in more detail and highlight some offers you might make.

Relevance

The relevance of the offer is most obviously expressed as the response rate. A higher response rate means higher relevance, although response can be influenced by other aspects of context.

Earlier, I suggested that the minimum response rate for offers-in-context should be 10%. The rationale is simple: it ensures we focus on making offers that matter to the customer and the business. Lower response rates don't just signal lower relevance but also higher intrusiveness and customer irritation. For some segments of customers, even a 10% response might still represent an unwelcome level of intrusiveness and irritation. The management of this can be baked into the offer generation process or managed within a CRM framework.

The relevance might be a straight-line relationship between the underlying event and the offer. A simple example: you purchased an airline ticket on your credit card, so you might require travel insurance. Additional analytics might also identify you've done three trips in the previous six months and might be better suited with an annual travel insurance plan. You could also build a predictive scorecard to pre-score customers for an annual policy. We can increase the relevance of the offer in various ways, both simple and complex.

The connection between the observed behaviour/event and the offer might be less obvious. In the new-mover example (from Chapter 9, "How to Pick Winners"), we generate a loan offer because the customer told us they were moving. How about a customer browsing online T&Cs for a product they already own? Does that mean an increased attrition risk and the need for a save offer?

You often need a little creativity to find an offer of high relevance given an observed behaviour, transaction, or event. Here's one astonishingly simple example.

Certain birthdays inevitably remind us about the relentless march of time; 30th, 40th or 50th birthdays are a good time to discuss long-term planning with a customer (for saving, investment, or insurance). Naturally, the 30th is not as effective as the 29th or the 31st—test it and you should see the difference. The beauty of these milestone birthdays is that the customer will already be thinking about their own mortality when your offer arrives... after the birthday, not before.

Timeliness

We intuitively understand that more recent data has the highest targeting relevance, greatest analytical impact and most predictive power (when compared with the same data from an older time period).

Look at any credit bureau risk score and there'll be variables like "number of searches for credit in the last 4 weeks". It's highly predictive of credit-stress. The same cannot be said of something like "number of searches for credit 12 to 24 months ago"; in isolation, probably not predictive at all.

Similarly, more recent customer behaviour is the most predictive of customer need, and therefore most indicative of likely response to offers satisfying that need. And if we do not recognise and satisfy the need, then someone else probably will; the offer is therefore time constrained.

Consider different perspectives on time. Figure 16.1 shows different ways to view events in time. This is not exhaustive, but it should illustrate four different perspectives and their relative importance. Many of the events listed could easily be used as basic event triggers—at least when you can get to the data.

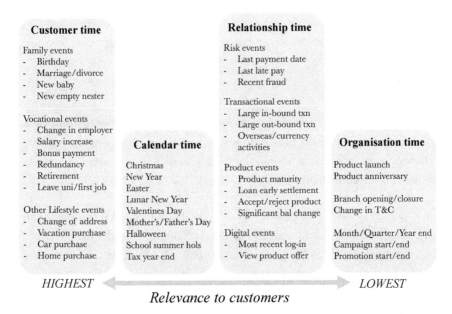

Figure 16.1 Perspectives on Time

Customer time events are personal, highly impactful on the customer and therefore of high relevance. Most significant life events should be captured here.

But we, as bankers, spend most of our working life in *organisation time* and whilst it might be uncomfortable to hear, customers do not care about organisational time. It never ceases to amaze me how often we subject customers to our campaign timetable. Shouldn't we be recognising events having relevance to the customer?

I've used all the events under relationship time (and more besides), and a fair few in the other categories too (including far too many than I care to mention under organisational time). Usually, the offers work because of relevance and timeliness; but they can also work as a simple opportunity to open a dialogue with the customer.

The vast majority of the listed events don't need a real-time recognition and response with an offer. Even a large inbound deposit can probably be left for a day or so, just to see whether the customer has a planned use for the funds.

When they occur, highly time-constrained opportunities demand an urgent response. Often these transient opportunities result from location specific impacts.

Location

Maybe it's a physical location: a store, a branch, a shopping mall or a street. You might have a promotion with a mall (or a store within it); the customer transacts somewhere in the mall; you spot the event and generate an offer about your promotion.

Alternatively, physical location can be mined from phone GPS data; it can be generated by your banking app using geofencing. Mobile providers are also offering more flexible location data services to third parties. I recently heard a fascinating story from the world of airline loyalty.

Obviously, airlines can see when loyalty programme members fly with them. They also know when a member flies on another carrier in their particular alliance (OneWorld, Star Alliance, and others). But the real smarts come with the help of telcos location data. Using this, an airline can identify when a member turns up in another country, even when they cannot see the flight details by other means.

Even the airline and flight flown can be estimated, using the time the member switches off/on their phone and matching to published schedules. This is incredibly powerful information—for identifying lost revenue, wallet share, price differentials, routing or timing black-spots. All generated through the creative use of location data.

You too can do out-of-the-box actions based on location information—however you derive it. I once introduced a trigger identifying an offshore customer performing a transaction in the local market. No offer was delivered to the customer; but a message was sent to that customer's local relationship manager, letting them know the customer was close.

Location context also means online stores are an obvious opportunity. Plain vanilla offers are easy but tend to be generic, e.g. "Convert the payment you just made into an instalment", "Get our XYZ co-brand card to earn double the rewards".

One of my credit card issuers has recently launched an online service with local supermarkets, and it's a great OIC opportunity. After payment and authorisation, I am presented with an offer which at its core is:

"Would you like to use reward points to offset part of the bill?"

The redemption cost is about 49bps; which translates to 10,205 card rewards points for a HK$50 rebate (about US$6.50). For some customers, the chance of a simple redemption holds allure; and delivers a significant financial upside to the card issuer since the redemption cost is relatively cheap. For others (like air mile junkies) the attraction is extremely low.

There's a possible third scenario to consider: is the offer convincing lower-level redeemers to burn points that would otherwise have expired? In such circumstances, the redemption cost to the issuer might actually increase.

So how to measure the net impact of the offer? The way we should analyse all campaigns:

- Don't consider the short-term performance in isolation. Examine longer-term behaviours too.

- Use test and control to measure true lifts (so don't make the offer to every eligible customer).

Hopefully, the offer is net positive for the issuer. It's certainly a great experience for some customers.

Offers like this are the tip of the iceberg, and analytics can significantly enhance the customisation of offers.

What about segmenting the target audience (using card BIN is the simplest) and differentiating offers based upon potential redemption cost savings, thus attempting to drive meaningful changes in customer behaviour? How about, changing the redemption rate each month to identify sensitivity? Maybe, personalising the offer in response to the individual customers historical redemption behaviours?

Channel

If the offer isn't urgent, then you can defer much of the channel allocation effort to your CRM engines. We'll deal with this in the next couple of chapters.

For urgent offers, channel allocation comprises much of the context and is critical to timely offer delivery.

If a customer's online and about to make a purchase, there's little point sending them an email or an SMS. The offer needs to be presented on-screen, and the mechanics should be seamless. Customer experience should not be negatively impacted. The offer should be viewed as a natural extension of the interaction.

In the offline world, if you're on the move, deployment options are limited—it's SMS or notification via mobile phone. Maybe an outbound call works, but it needs to be a significant offer to offset the intrusion.

Time Revisited

A few behaviours require real-time recognition and offer generation; but most can survive a day (or more) before action. There are yet more where a behaviour triggers an offer weeks, or even months, later.

Any time you lose a significant balance (card revolve or banking deposit) the competitor destination is usually identifiable from settlement files. You can also infer the likely competitor promotional offer and duration. Armed with this intel, you can generate offers timed for delivery at the end of the competitor promotion, attempting to reacquire the balance.

I discussed such balance reacquisition approaches in the previous chapter on retention. A word of caution, however—it's a slippery slope. These balances are akin to "hot money", continuously seeking the best available market rate. Your success in reacquiring each balance might be short-lived; but any strategic imperative driving the reacquisition effort might be considered more important.

Implementation Challenges

Offers-in-context represent a very different approach to traditional lead generation.

There can be issues of "process", you're moving from few, lower responding campaigns, to many, higher responding campaigns. The daily volume may be small, but over time it adds up. And complexity can be managed (we'll consider how in the upcoming CRM discussion).

Some events listed in Figure 16.1 cannot be recognised using explicit data; although they might be inferred from subsequent transactions merchant (payments, deposits, withdrawals). For many events, the data does exist; make sure you are loading it to your analytics data platform in a timely manner.

Don't forget, it's small numbers of affected customers and large numbers of different offers-in-context. But it's more complicated than spotting the event, generating an offer and communicating to the customer. An important element of context is the history of offers made to each customer. To understand this in more detail, we need to consider customer relationship management.

CHAPTER 17

CRM and Early Engagement

Customer relationship management (CRM) is an approach to managing customer communications across the organisation. A comprehensive implementation might cover not just sales and marketing, but also customer service, operations, and any other source of customer communication.

For our purposes, we will focus on core marketing campaigns and offers-in-context. Within this more limited scope, a CRM implementation should have three objectives:

- **Integration.** All campaigns are subjected to the same set of business rules. The aim is to deliver the most appropriate (however defined) campaigns and offers to each customer.

- **Coherence.** Using previous offer history to ensure the customer sees a sensible and logical succession of offers, not a random mess of unrelated and/or inappropriate campaigns.

- **Optimisation.** Through the use of contact history, targeting analytics and continuous testing to squeeze the best possible results from each contact.

A full CRM implementation will probably mean a substantial overhaul of existing campaign approaches. Targeting analytics need to be developed, business processes must be changed, campaign complexity will rise dramatically, and the volume of campaigns will increase significantly, particularly when incorporating multiple offers-in-context.

Taken from this perspective, CRM might seem overly complicated, expensive and risky. But...

- You don't need to do everything at once. Take it slow and in manageable "bite-sized" chunks. Start with early engagement, introduce a few offers-in-context and then gradually incorporate each core marketing campaign.

- You need not buy an off-the-shelf solution (although you can). I've reviewed many vendor solutions over time, but have always ended up building the solution with my own teams. It's not technically difficult, but it needs to be modular and requires good process design.

- And you don't have to implement a total solution; a partial solution can deliver significant business performance increases. There's a minimum set of requirements, but that's not too onerous.

So, with these points in mind, the place to start is the early engagement phase of the customer lifecycle, because:

- It's easy to "ring fence" customers, isolating them from other mainstream marketing activities (which are probably mostly within the development phase of the lifecycle); and

- Relatively small customer volumes are affected (at least compared to the existing customer base). It is therefore easier to allow "proof-of-concept" testing on these activities.

Organisations often don't much try to treat new customers in a special way; it introduces avoidable complexity, particularly where multiple products must be fulfilled. Welcome processes are mostly operationally focused; getting the cards despatched and maybe top-tier retail proposition customers will get a call from their relationship manager.

The focus is usually on getting the new customers integrated with the existing portfolio as fast as possible. *This is exactly the wrong thing to do; you should be recognising that these new customers are special.*

One notable exception to this, although it's not universal, is using the credit card activation as an opportunity to sell something—balance transfer, credit insurance, and payment protection are typical. It's fast, it's simple, and needs limited analytics. But early engagement has so much more potential.

What am I advocating? What should you be trying to do with early engagement? Why should we upset the status quo?

> **The active engagement of new customers will build and reinforce desirable customer behaviour. Success will typically set the customer on a higher usage trajectory than that achieved from the customer's self-directed activities.**

But the approach introduces complexity, and it forces consideration of the customer experience and journey.

Here's an example. Consider the roll-out of a new CRM engagement approach; there's one product, and we want to execute a particular marketing treatment to new customers in each of their first six months. The approach will "go live" in January and initially operate on all customers booked in the previous month. The growth in campaign numbers is shown in Figure 17.1.

January	February	March		June
M1 offer to Dec booked	M1 offer to Jan booked	M1 offer to Feb booked	...	M1 offer to May booked
	M2 offer to Dec booked	M2 offer to Jan booked		M2 offer to Apr booked
		M3 offer to Dec booked		M3 offer to Mar booked
				M4 offer to Feb booked
				M5 offer to Jan booked
				M6 offer to Dec booked

Figure 17.1 Possible CRM Engagement Roll-out

January is our roll-out month and has just the first month offer (M1) to those customers booked last month (Dec). In February, we need to have the M1 offer to the new customers booked in January; and the M2 offer for the December booked customers. Each month, we add another activity until it reaches a steady state in June; six offers are then running every month.

It's important to recognise this is an artificial view, since:

- You probably wouldn't want to hit all customers every month. That's a little too intensive for some, but you can test for this.

    Maybe you don't communicate on a monthly basis; weekly or even daily might be more appropriate. One approach I've successfully used was the delivery of multiple "welcome messages" in the early weeks, each introducing or expanding particular product features.

- You need to think about how to measure performance lifts. It's unrealistic to have a control group for every treatment and every cell, but some measurement is necessary.

- The assumption is one offer per cohort per month. In reality, the system is learning from month to month. There are customers who have accepted or rejected the M1 offer, they might have different M2 offers, which can also be accepted or rejected. You could visualise the complete six months as a tree of possibilities. At each node, a two-way split is made on whether the customer accepted the offer.

This complexity forces you to take a lifecycle view when considering marketing actions. What makes sense as a third offer to a customer who accepted the first offer and declined the second? Is the third offer different for a customer who declined the first but accepted the second? Review each significant customer journey through the engagement process and ensure the offers are appropriate. It isn't as daunting as it might appear; and you really learn to appreciate the customer experience.

Credit Cards Early Engagement

Figure 17.2 shows an approach for credit cards. This is broadly based on real results, but is a highly simplified view of the solution that emerged after many months of testing different offer sequences.

An upfront behaviour estimation divides all new customers as either likely transactor or revolver. Once the welcome and activation phase is out of the way, three offers are made, at MOB 1, 3 and 5. Obviously, customers who have previously accepted an offer are excluded at each stage. In reality, they would receive different offers, but I'm keeping it simple.

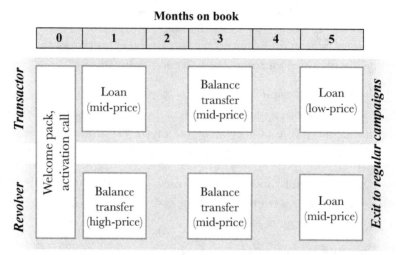

Figure 17.2 Example Cards Early Engagement Actions

Pricing and offers vary for both transactors and revolvers, exploring possible customer need and price sensitivity. The loan offered is within the customer's card line.

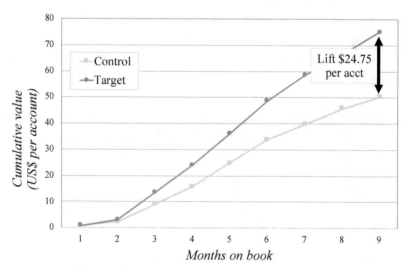

Figure 17.3 Credit Card Engagement Impact

Figure 17.3 shows the results. The control group (representing half the customers) got the traditional treatment. The targets went through the structured engagement process. Comparison between the two groups shows a clear performance lift. We are comparing like-with-like; same type

158

of customers, same time-period, but different treatments. MOB 1 offers have a customer value impact from the end of MOB 2 onwards.

The results exhibit a near 50% customer value (net revenue or gross profit) improvement, albeit against a fairly benign control (some plain vanilla offers at, essentially, random times). Complete results showed lifts for both transactors and revolvers; not shown here.

General Banking Early Engagement

A similar approach also works for new general banking customers. The actions shown in Figure 17.4 represent an interim stage—it wasn't the first approach we tried, nor the last.

Different approaches were applied to different customer segments, this example impacted the upscale proposition—requiring customers to have a minimum of c. US$150,000 in total balances (or face a high monthly fee). If customers are significantly below balance at MOB2, specific remedial actions are taken.

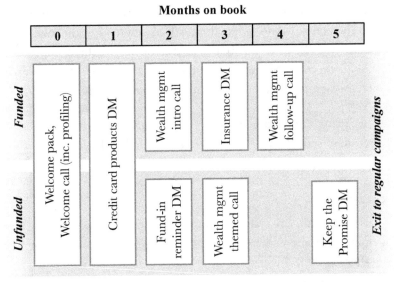

Figure 17.4 General Banking Engagement Actions

Calls are made by the customer's relationship manager (RM). Extensive use is made of high-quality direct mail (DM) material to introduce products.

This is a highly simplified view, but it serves to demonstrate the basic principles of the approach.

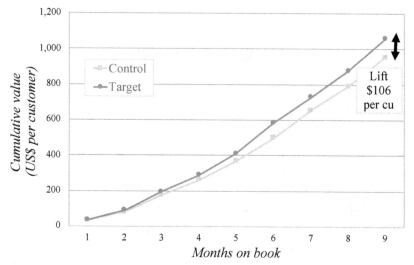

Figure 17.5 General Banking Engagement Impact

Results are shown in Figure 17.5. A US$106 increase represents an 11% lift versus the control. And unlike the cards example, the control here was actively targeted. Lift was attributed to the more structured approach to engagement, executed consistently across all customers in the target group, with increased emphasis on securing initial account funds in.

Lower tier propositions use email exclusively, and a different set of offers. The products, sequencing, and channel use should be tailored to the audience.

Conclusions

New customers are special. Customised actions throughout the early engagement period can set customers on a higher usage trajectory than might otherwise be achieved.

The approach is particularly useful where the customer relationship is relatively remote (e.g. digital-only).

The examples here are simplistic. In practice, each month needs to consider the history of offers made and accepted, learning and adapting with experience. It's a tree of actions and outcomes, and each customer traverses the tree in their early months, their precise route decided by the offers made and products taken at each stage.

Broad themes ("customer journeys") can be embedded within particular routes through the tree of possibilities—with specific business objectives (like fully funding a new upscale account, or building a credit card balance).

Further operational considerations:

- Using customer value to measure performance removes ambiguity. It's a clear and unequivocal measure.

- Decide on an evaluation period. In the examples above, structured engagement actions covered the first six months and evaluation was done until month 9. You could extend the evaluation to ensure the performance difference is sustained.

Implementing this initial step of CRM is remarkably straightforward, needs limited analytics, and delivers excellent performance lifts.

CHAPTER 18

CRM Across the Customer Lifecycle

Any CRM implementation is worthy of a book in its own right, and we can only cover so much in a couple of chapters. What I'm trying to articulate here is a partial solution that captures a significant amount of the sales and marketing benefits of CRM, but without major expense on technology development, integration and process changes.

Those benefits can be significant. In the last chapter, we saw customer value lifts of up to 54% for early engagement. For development actions lifts in response rates can be even greater.

Getting started with CRM for early engagement is technically straightforward. More importantly, there is limited risk to "business as usual" marketing and sales approaches—it's a gradual roll out to a relatively small number of customers. The barriers to initial implementation are very low.

However, once a customer exits early engagement and joins the mainstream portfolio, things become more problematic. Now we're talking about a fundamental change in approach and many affected customers.

But, whilst implementing CRM driven sales and marketing represents a significant change from typical approaches, it shouldn't involve uncertainty and risk. It's a natural evolution in your approaches; moving you ever closer to the recognition and fulfilment of customer need and the application of analytics to drive "next best offer" targeting for optimising marketing and sales activity.

This chapter will outline a step-by-step approach to implementing a partial CRM solution, gradually increasing in sophistication and complexity. Even the simplest steps can identify and address customer need... and unlock significant value.

1	**Contact Protocols**	The rules governing frequency of customer contact, to which all campaigns and promotions must comply. If you only implement one component of CRM, do this.
2	**Basic OIC**	The simplest offers-in-context don't need sophisticated technology or processes, just slightly different thinking.
3	**Offer Rotation**	Doing the right activities continuously throughout the year. At steady state, you'll have smooth volumes, increased response, and less volatility.
4	**Batch OIC**	Unlocking significant opportunities from transactional events with minor technical development.
5	**Offer Optimisation**	Supporting multiple campaigns, products and offers using targeting analytics and "next best offer" logic
6	**Real-time OIC**	Usually, a significant challenge for technology and processes, but with a big payout.

Figure 18.1 Evolving CRM Implementation Steps

Softly, softly, catchy monkey. Take it step by step; at each stage learning and adjusting. Maybe launch and develop with a subsegment of customers; or with specific channels or products.

My preferred approach is always credit cards first, then general banking. As you'll see when we expand the steps, there's an excellent reason for this... CRM for credit cards is usually more straightforward.

Step 1: Contact Protocols

Access to customers for marketing purposes must be controlled. You can't allow multiple businesses, products and functions to bombard customers with offers. There must be ground rules. The most basic rules should cover contact frequency and cross product access; these are covered by *contact protocols*.

With a wide variety of potential channels, some with a lead distribution cost of close to zero, there's an inevitable temptation for the marketer or product owner to max out the volume.

Resist that temptation. Do not succumb to the allure of shovelling out a couple of hundred thousand (or more) extra SMS, emails or notifications. Just because the delivery cost is miniscule, it does not mean there aren't wider business economic impacts and costs.

For any channel, when you over-contact a group of customers with the same offer, you will see *contact fatigue*. It is evidenced by a fall in the response rate because:

- Repeating the same message over and over becomes less compelling; and/or,

- Once a customer has responded, they are no longer within the target population; consequently, the population is less target rich. There is an underlying replacement rate (newly eligible customers joining the pool, for example). But once your responses exceed replacements, the response rate will fall.

Other damaging results from over-contact include:

- An increase in customers opting-out or unsubscribing from marketing and sales communications. They have become fed-up with the volume of unsolicited, unwanted and/or inappropriate offers.

- Over-contacting on one channel can have consequences for other channels. A customer might receive their 22nd SMS of the week, decide enough-is-enough and opt out from all channels.

- Higher levels of attrition. If the customer "blames" the product, then it might be just product level attrition, but if the customer blames the bank, the total relationship could be unwinding.

A walk-through of a real-world protocol appears in the appendices. Figure 18.2 shows an extremely simple protocol example.

Channel contact maximums	1-day	7-day	30-day
In-bound service	1	2	4
Direct mail	1	2	3
Email	1	2	3
SMS	1	2	3
App notifications	2	4	6
Telemarketing	1	1	2

Figure 18.2 A Simple Contact Protocol

Protocols apply for active channels; they are less relevant for passive channels[3] like social media and online (in-bound service is included above because the impact on customer experience can be significant).

There are limits assigned on the contact volumes per day, week and month. You rarely have a single protocol. Normally, a separate protocol should apply for different customer segments and products, but there's always a customer-level protocol which is the over-arching boss.

In reality, setting limits on communication volumes is initially rather arbitrary. We don't know the tipping point (what is "too much") and it's difficult to test for, particularly in the short-term—although you can watch out for movement in the unsubscribe rate for notifications and email.

Spend time investigating the issues, consider the customers perspective, and fine tune the detailed settings as experience informs.

---

[3] Communications to an active channel are always delivered (or at least attempted). A passive channel requires waiting for the customer to show up before delivery. Initially discussed in Chapter 3.

Step 2: Basic Offer-in-Context Generation

There are a few different ways to generate offers-in-context. Let's start with the most straightforward.

Some events don't need sophisticated technology and processes, they can be simply identified in advance—things like birthdays, product maturities, offer expiries, and approaching loan settlement. Offers that exploit these events can usually be processed in tandem with the core lead production. Either:

- The customer gets an OIC instead of the business-as-usual offer; or

- The customer gets both an OIC and the business-as-usual (BAU) offer, but on different channels. This works when the offers are different and not for the same product. Note that (a) the OIC is usually the highest priority, so should occupy the best responding channel; and (b) the BAU offer does tend to become somewhat redundant.

This is a clean and simple way to start your offers-in-context development. No major re-engineering of data collection, lead generation or marketing processes is required.

Step 3: Core Campaign Offer Rotation

Core campaigns are those that drive incremental business and are run multiple times across the year. The generation of these business-as-usual core marketing campaigns is usually a large monthly (or some other period) production process.

A separate CRM process should be run to support core campaigns for each major customer base, maybe one for credit cards and one for general banking (and sometimes one for SME). The processes should operate independently and be bound by contact protocols.

Let's consider two very different approaches to CRM based lead generation. The first (usually the more straightforward approach) uses offer rotation and works extremely effectively with credit cards.

To illustrate the approach, consider a scenario where credit card *core programs* are about balance build, and maybe a bit of insurance cross-selling. In some circumstances (and if you have the patience), balance build can be achieved through spend stimulation programs. More immediately, it can be via balance transfers (and their equivalents) or instalment programs.

Spend stimulation efforts rarely fit the core criteria, e.g. the offer might have a limited time period or apply to a limited audience. But if you have enough of them across the year or you developed a generic whole-year program, then it can be classified as a core program.

There's also an entire class of spend offers best delivered via offers-in-context, because either: they are specific anti-attrition measures, or they are location and/or time sensitive.

For this example, we will assume just two core programs: balance build and insurance cross-sell. General spend stimulation campaigns are therefore outside the **CRM** framework (such ad hoc programs have to comply with a few ground rules but are perfectly allowable).

With only a couple of offers, the easy way to implement the production is to divide the base into two equal parts and flip-flop between the two offers. But a two-month cycle is too frequent for repetition (resulting in falling response). Three months usually delivers a more sustainable response rate; therefore, the customer base needs to be divided into three equal parts.

	Month 1	Month 2	Month 3	Month 1	
Group A	Balance build	Insurance	Rested	Balance build	
Group B	Insurance	Rested	Balance build	Insurance	*etc.*
Group C	Rested	Balance build	Insurance	Rested	

Figure 18.3 Rotating Offer Example

In figure 18.3 we've introduced a third option, where customers are rested, i.e. they receive no offers. You can use the rested month for other purposes, maybe a cross-sell of retail banking, for example. The point is to give sufficient time for response to recover for core credit card programs.

As a general rule, do not use models for targeting balance build activities to the entire base. Such models age rapidly, and they quickly settle into a behaviour where broadly the same subset of the total customer base is presented each month as potential targets. If you repeatedly target the same group, you will get contact fatigue, response rates will fall, and you must contact more and more customers to reach your goal. Plus, the subset the model wants to target are likely to be revolvers, who will (pretty much) take any offer at any discounted price.

Stand back and think again. If you keep targeting a subset, say 20%, of the base, then you continuously ignore opportunities in the other 80%. The goal must surely be to make an economically viable offer to as many customers as possible, whilst ensuring acceptable response rates.

An "off the shelf" segmentation specifically for credit card balance build is considered in the appendices. I've applied it in multiple markets, it doesn't age and delivers excellent results.

It is important to recognise rotating offers across months will work for other types of core offers, not just balance build.

In an offer rotation scheme, it's often unnecessary to employ tight analytical targeting for insurance. But if required, such targeting is easy. Generic "risk averse" models can target several insurance products; but higher predictiveness can be achieved be developing targeting for individual products. As mentioned previously, the easiest approach is to offer low cost/high perceived value products; once the customer bites, pull them up the value chain. Don't get greedy; don't try selling the high value products immediately.

Offer rotation approaches deliver stability—of target volumes, responses and sales. Effort can be concentrated on adopting champion/challenger approaches to improving performance.

Step 4: Batch Offers-in-Context

Slightly more complicated is the generation of offers intra-month, i.e. outside the business-as-usual offer generation process. Weekly or daily processing can pick up on particular transactions, aggregate changes in balances, etc. Of course, you need the data, either as a weekly/daily warehouse update or as raw feeds after the day-end batch has completed. Although the tech required here is pretty basic, the results can be spectacular—after all, offers are in response to specific behaviours or situations; they are timely, meaningful and relevant.

But there is a complication here: how to deal with the BAU offers that have already been generated? There's a danger of over-contacting the customer, but also the potential for conflicting messages/offers. For some channels, if you can recall (or delete) the BAU offer, it can be replaced with the new OIC—particularly useful in passive channels (e.g. web display, or in-bound service) where the BAU offer hasn't yet been made. For other channels you need to consider whether you should still generate the OIC, or maybe relegate delivery to a lower priority channel.

You could just assume that any identified offer-in-context is a higher priority that a BAU offer. That would be easy and relatively simple to implement. A more nuanced approach needs to compare all existing offers and consider which one (if any) to replace with the OIC. To do this, you need a central repository of all the current offers for a customer, with deployment details and status. You can probably survive without it for batch OIC, but any additional sophistication does need it.

Step 5: Core Campaigns Optimisation

More core products are potentially available to offer a banking customer, so complexity can increase. When dealing with more than a few offers, you need to use increased sophistication to select the most appropriate customer/offer combinations.

You could restrict the number of core offers, maybe to three or four, and then adopt a rotation approach (similar to cards). The process would then repeatedly cycle through the offers. Don't forget we can augment that with further offer sophistication using OICs rather than core programs.

But after four products, the viability of offer rotation inevitably starts to fall. If you're not rotating offers, you need to consider all the different potential offers and determine which ones to make, and on which channels. When comparing the offers, there are a few important considerations:

- Every customer needs to be assessed for every available core offer and allocated an expected response rate. If you don't have advanced analytics for a core program, use a proxy response rate (either at the total campaign level or at a finer resolution if available).

- It is important that the response rates of different campaigns are comparable. If you developed one piece of targeting analytics using email response, another from branch calls, and another from direct mail, then you need to normalise them. If you don't, then an unfair comparison is being made.

   You need to re-weight all estimated responses to compensate and normalise around a single channel (usually the one used most often). If there's no comparative data, it needs to be generated using a single offer/campaign across multiple channels. As discussed in Chapter 11, "Measuring Campaign Effectiveness", response is defined as a sale.

- You also need to down weight expected response if the customer has been contacted with the same offer in recent months. If you have no precise data (from previous observation) then a good place to start is: reduce expected response by 50% if contacted in the last month; 25% if contacted in two months.

   The alternative is simply to ensure that no offer is delivered to a customer more than once every three months.

- Rank order all the offers for each individual customer and allocate to channel(s) subject to contact protocols and customer channel preferences (we'll discuss these shortly).

You don't need to "process" every campaign together. Generate an initial state using one or multiple campaigns. Subsequent campaigns can then be run against this state to determine whether specific offer/channel combinations should be replaced.

This undoubtedly looks complicated, particularly in comparison with most existing execution. Yes, there is additional complexity, but the performance lifts will justify the investment. The effort is (mostly) a one-time deal involving process redesign and developing modular components to apply scores, rank order, and make selections.

Response or value to prioritise an offer?

Let's start with a confession. I've spent a fair amount of my career designing and implementing increasingly sophisticated (and complicated) CRM solutions. And I now think some of that time was probably wasted in the pursuit of marginal performance improvements that came at too high an additional development cost (when measured by intellectual effort and implementation hours).

Having spent many years and much effort developing revenue optimisation approaches attempting to balance response versus revenue, I'm finally back to where I started. Response rules!

Consider an offer with a 1% response rate delivering a $2,000 revenue per response. That's an *offer efficiency* of $20 per contact (response multiplied by revenue). It represents the amount of money we make per contact. There's probably additional interest from a further 1% of the contacts, but with no sales. Now consider an offer with a 50% response rate and delivering $10 per response. The offer efficiency for the second offer is $5.

Which do you choose? I'd choose the second offer and take 50% response, for two reasons:

1. In the short-term, I won't make as much money, but I've satisfied a greater customer need. Customers who accepted the offer are now more engaged.

2. For everyone who accepted, there's probably another who was tempted by the offer, so we also have a halo of goodwill.

And if that first offers 1% response rate were higher, I might even consider making that offer in the following month, but only on a relatively non-intrusive channel, like email, direct mail, or web display, and only if there was no better offer available.

Step 6: Real-time OIC

At the highest level of complexity is the real-time detection and actioning of events. Detecting the event will probably require some technology development. For credit cards, you can piggy-back the transaction authorisation traffic for a quick fix. For retail banking transactions, you might be able to exploit existing fraud or money laundering detection systems. If you've got nothing to leverage, then development from scratch can be arduous and likely not worth the investment in the short-term—remember that you can get a long way by exploiting the overnight batch approach.

One notable exception is the real-time support of offer generation for third-party websites and location dependent events. It's unavoidable functionality for the near future. But how smart do you want it to be?

A relatively unintelligent approach would use generic offers, e.g. customer enters geofenced region indicating a shopping mall, therefore communicate spending promotion via an app notification. The next level of sophistication would update your worldview to save details of the offer made to the customer. Even more useful would be a dynamically generated offer: the app requests an offer when the customer enters the geofenced area and the CRM system responds with the most appropriate offer of those available.

This is getting quite sophisticated. But remember, the first steps in implementing offers-in-context are easy. You can build additional sophistication over time.

Allocating Offers to Channels

In a sophisticated CRM engine, there's an offer repository representing all the offers applicable for a customer at any moment in time. The CRM engine should handle offers as they are generated for each customer—

assigning expected response rates and offer priorities, and then updating the offer palette. Offers should be picked from the offer palette and deployed to a channel on demand.

Note: Individual channel deployment approaches depend on your infrastructure (including tech and processes). The best deployment is in real-time; the worst, an overnight batch dump, maybe losing competitive advantage.

In allocating offers to channels, there are multiple considerations:

- *Contactability.* It's important to identify every returned mailing, bounced email, and disconnected phone number. Ensure there's a process to capture the information, incorporate that into channel allocation, and generate actions to source updated data—in-bound service calls and web display work well, and test customer incentives.

  Worst case: you keep sending offers that never get delivered.

- *Offer rules*. Every offer should have a variety of meta-data. This might include the offer description, expiry date, eligible channels, channel priority order, and a generic offer priority (reflecting the offer importance, relative to others)

- *Customer preferences*. Gone are the days when customers had a single choice: whether to be opted-in or opted-out of marketing communications. These days almost everyone now offers separate channel opt-in/out choices (for direct mail, e-mail, voice or SMS), and the ability to make changes on-line, plus app settings to manage notifications and subscriptions.

  Where a customer is actively opting-out of one channel, but remaining opted-in for another, they are sharing one aspect of their channel preferences.

- *Time/location sensitivity*. Highly time constrained offers (including location driven) must use the customer's mobile phone; which means SMS, app notification or a voice call.

You could handle this sensitivity separately, but it's best rolled into the offer rules above, i.e. set applicable channels as required and assign a very high priority for the offer.

- **_Multi-channel characteristics_**. When you want to get a single message out, populate it across multiple channels. If you have a limited palette of offers for a particular customer, this can be a useful reinforcement.

  Try to measure the effectiveness using a single channel first, before committing additional multi-channel complexity; then you can measure the lift between single and multi-channel.

- **_Response rates_**. Once the factors above are handled, the final allocation mechanism uses comparative response rates between offers.

  There is always a hierarchy of channel responsiveness, irrespective of the offer being made; some are always better than others. The allocation rule is simple: for each customer, allocate the most responsive offers to the most responsive channels.

The allocation of offers to channels should also be subject to a minimum response rate. No offers should be deployed where the expected response rate is below the minimum. My suggestions are shown in Figure 18.3.

Priority	Channel	Min. response
1	Relationship selling	8%
2	Telemarketing	4%
3	Direct mail	2%
4	Email	2%
5	Notification	2%
6	SMS	1%
7	Web display	1%

Figure 18.3 Minimum Response by Channel

Offers targeted using paid search and social are not included. Such activities are primarily used for new customer acquisition; not existing customer offers.

These suggested minimums are not based on campaign economics. I'm sure there are many campaigns that would find lower response rates economically acceptable. I'm proposing these minimums based on customer experience and expectations. Nevertheless, a 1% response for SMS implies just one person in a hundred was interested in the offer, 99 were not. Web display is less of an issue, since it's passive and relatively non-intrusive.

There's also an opportunity cost: the lost revenue from being unable to make an alternative offer. If you've "filled up" your channels with low-responding offers, then you might be limiting opportunities for higher responding offers.

Customer Relationship Management Systems: Buy or Build?

The steps outlined above are not a full CRM solution. They represent a low-cost/high return approach to capturing some low-hanging-fruit when identifying opportunities and populating to channels.

A full CRM system solution might comprise aspects of marketing campaign generation, sales force management, lead management, business reporting, and more. It might also have separate components to manage social media, mobile, servicing, etc. There are some highly sophisticated offerings out there, and barriers to implementation are at an all-time low.

But there can be significant expense.

Of course, it's not just about the expense, it's also about the return. The financial justifications for a CRM system are usually based on assumed improvements in customer retention and sales (with a halo of benefits in customer experience).

Let's look at things in slightly more detail. Performance lifts (for improved retention and increased sales) can come from three potential sources:

1. The CRM system alone; you wouldn't be able to get the lifts without it.

2. Analytical insights alone (including the generation of customer offers), and the results don't need the CRM system, they are also realisable by different delivery mechanics.

3. A combination of both, where it is the unique nature of the analytics and CRM systems working together delivering the performance lifts.

It's surprising just how much benefit is achievable using analytical insights alone.

Indeed, every large organisation I've worked with has used a homegrown approach: analytically driven lead generation, hand-off files to the various channel deployment tools, and a front-end lead management system for manned channels.

There are obviously other benefits from CRM systems (particularly when coupled with marketing automation tools) and these solutions will continue to evolve. The relative importance of analytical insights alone may well decline and change the cost/benefit calculus.

CRM Wrap-up

I never intended to articulate a complete CRM solution here; it isn't even possible without the inclusion of servicing and operational messages. But I have provided a mechanism to build out capabilities that increase integration, coherence and optimisation in sales/marketing communications, whilst also recognising genuine customer need.

The effort implied in the foregoing discussion might appear daunting, particularly to newcomers. Try not to focus on the total complexity but look at single components and consider how they might be implemented. Start small and build out. You need not move straight to a complete solution; gradually deliver different components and build out coverage.

Your effort will be worth it in the long run.

PART IV

EXECUTION CONSIDERATIONS

"Never confuse motion with action"
Benjamin Franklin, Founding Father of the US (Jan 1706—Apr 1790)

"He uses statistics as a drunken man uses lamp posts –
for support rather than illumination"
Andrew Lang, Scottish writer (Mar 1844—Jul 1912)

CHAPTER 19

Structure and People

There is no "one size fits all" solution to how the analytics function should be structured. I've built functions from scratch, and I've inherited existing teams. I've dealt with smart and capable tech teams who truly understand the data and access requirements of an analytics team; but I've also encountered a few who are less able. I've worked for mono-line credit cards and full-service banks. And I've seen massive support and enthusiasm for analytics, but also the challenges inherent in less supportive environments where you're trying to build credibility.

But despite these different start-points, a few key specialisms are common to every end-point team structure:

- *Information & Infrastructure Management.* Oversight of data provisioning, platforms, tools and automation.

- *Business Analysis.* Interfacing analytics with the business.

- *Advanced Analytics.* Developing and deploying predictive capabilities.

At various times my analytics remit has also included: market research (and "customer insights"), Risk/Credit MIS, sales commission calculation, database building, customer balance credit/debit adjustments and all manner of bizarre operational reporting.

Suffice to say, some of these activities are more appropriate and acceptable than others, and we'll come to that in the next chapter. Right now, let's expand on the remit of the three key specialisms identified above.

Information and Infrastructure Management

IIM represents a centralised pool of expertise in the more technical areas supporting analytics delivery. Responsibilities are listed below.

Platforms and tools i.e. the mechanisms to access the data and the software used. This covers all day-to-day maintenance, periodic updates, investigation, evaluation and installation of new tools, and liaising with technology teams.

Data management and development*.* Existing data needs to be actively managed. Bank operational systems are upgraded, new products are launched, new functionality is developed; all impacting the existing data environment. Responsibility for continuous data improvement falls to the IIM team, including the expansion of data coverage of internal operational systems, increasing the speed of refresh (working towards real-time) and the sourcing of external data as necessary.

Automation*.* I am a passionate advocate for massive, industrial scale automation of analytical and reporting tasks. I have had great success in driving productivity improvements using automation. Critical success factors include:

- An automation-friendly data architecture, possibly including data-marts specifically designed to support automation tasks.

- Standardised deliverables, including common definitions, template reports, and parameterisation.

All regular basic reporting and management information (daily, weekly, monthly) delivered by analytics should be automated; none should need manual involvement. Streamline and standardise requirements to facilitate automation.

Governance and control oversight should reside within IIM, including internal audits and self-assessments. Responsibilities should include data access controls, data management, and data security as necessary to ensure best practice. The IIM remit is generally internal (not client) focused; that business independence makes such activities a natural fit.

Business Analysis

Way back in Chapter 1, business engagement was identified as a critical success factor when building analytics capabilities. For engagement, business analysis is "where the rubber hits the road".

This function is the interface between analytics and the business. Typically, there should be a separate business analysis team for each major client group. Each analyst group needs a full understanding of the business context, history, products and goals.

All the business's key requests for analytical and CRM support come via their lead business analyst, who might also self-identify analytical opportunities.

It takes a special person to be a business analyst. They need a deep knowledge of the business they support, and the client business team should consider the analyst integral to success. They need to lead a team of more junior analysts who help deliver the work. The business analyst translates the client requirements into an analytical action plan, deploys the resources to complete the work, and ultimately delivers the results.

Make no mistake, these folks aren't just business savvy and numerate. They also need to deliver analysis themselves; they must be excellent communicators and they are the standard bearers for analytics out there in the wider business.

Advanced Analytics

This should cover predictive and prescriptive analytics. The business analysis teams should deliver data mining and other descriptive analysis wherever possible; that's where the business and product expertise lives.

This team will be small, maybe one or two persons initially. Here's why:

- An analyst can produce around six advanced projects in a year (anti-attrition, cross-sell, up-sell models, and the like).

- Each model ages and becomes less effective as the underlying population changes and the market environment evolves. Typically, models should be replaced once they have lost sufficient predictive power. Let's assume the lifetime to be 18 months.

- So, an analyst can support a steady state of continuous development for around nine models. That's a reasonably large number; most businesses would probably be hard-pressed to identify nine predictive analytics opportunities for immediate use.

This is a simple perspective; models are run each month (at least) and performance must be tracked, and aging monitored. More resources are needed, but it will not be a large team.

The rationale for centralisation is simple: it's a high-end skill set, it should not be dispersed across the business analysis units.

Other Functional Areas

Better resourced bank analytics functions have options for more specialisation. Here are a few possibilities.

Digital Banking

Three key types of analytical support are required for digital banking (including the bank website and app). They are:

- Basic website and app metrics (logins, views, etc). Fodder for automation.

- Search engine optimisation and display placement (including programmatic), primarily for new customer acquisition. This is very different to the typical business, marketing and sales analytics; it's a highly specialised discipline. Larger organisations will typically develop in-house expertise, others will use digital agencies.

- Existing customer development via (a) website banners, pop-ups, modals, etc; and, (b) app real estate and notifications. The media might be state-of-the-art, but effective use has a shared DNA with other media: test and control, champion/challenger, attribute testing, and integrated messaging (across all channels and customer interactions).

CRM/List Production

Better resourced banks should consider a dedicated CRM team (or dedicated list production team if there's no CRM implementation). If not, the customer communications should be delivered by the same team that does performance tracking and data mining for that customer group.

I've seen customer communication lists delivered by marketing, Risk Management and even IT. I've seen 36-page system development requests just to produce a basic customer list. Typical problems include: poor campaign design, rudimentary results tracking, weak contact protocol adherence, and falling response rates.

Centralisation within the analytics group exploits scale advantage, and usually dramatically improves executional excellence and communication integration between campaigns and business groups.

Sales Incentives

I mentioned the challenges of sales incentive calculations a while ago. If these activities are supported, then responsibility should reside with a single nominated individual within the analytics group. Life will be challenging for around a week every month-end (longer at quarter- and year-end). Position the role as a "rite of passage" and after (say) twelve months the mantle falls to someone else (who should shadow the lead for a few months prior to handover).

What Makes a Good Analyst?

Whenever I am in discussions about big data and analytics, this is the question I am asked most often.

It's not easy to answer. As the foregoing discussion shows, there are multiple functional roles, some more aligned with IT, others with statistics, and others still with business management. Certain roles lend themselves well to individual (rather than team) effort; others demand high levels of interaction across internal teams or with business partners. So, in any analytics organisation there should be a place for many personality types and a variety of ways to contribute.

Here's my answer to the "good analyst" question.

First, a few obvious points:

- IIM analysts have an affinity with traditional IT roles and skills. If they are working on automation projects, then a good starting point is expertise in Excel macros and Visual Basic. As you get further into unstructured data, experience in text analysis and fuzzy matching will become increasingly useful.

- Advanced analytics requires technical skills in predictive modelling (typically regression and decision trees). These days that is most usefully augmented by experience of more esoteric predictive techniques (variants on scorecards and trees) and maybe neural nets and artificial intelligence. You need solid statistics knowledge.

- Business analysts need technical skills, most obviously programming—which is probably SAS and SQL for most banks, but we are getting more adventurous with Python, R, etc.

  The level of stats needed is fairly basic, and easily acquired—sample sizing, significance testing, etc. And, as articulated earlier, communication skills and interpersonal skills are essential.

The stark reality is that analytical success is rarely assessed on how good the models are, or how much report automation has been achieved, or the quality and timeliness of information. These are the "icing on the cake".

What really matters is the level of engagement with the business. The higher the engagement, the higher the likelihood that analytics is being applied in the right areas, and in the right ways.

Success therefore rests primarily with the business analysts and their ability to engage with the business. Interpersonal skills aside, their understanding of business context drives that engagement. And context learnt with competitors can be very useful, refreshing internal understanding of market dynamics and consumer behaviours.

There's a bunch of other stuff I could list for any analytics role, the most important of which (and I will often compromise technical skills for) is a love of problem and puzzle solving—they'll have to do a lot of that.

Team Management No Brainers

The quality of analytics leadership is most obviously expressed in the attrition rate of the team. Don't be fobbed off with excuses like, "It's unavoidable, it's a hot skill-set/market/environment out there". Attrition is mostly avoidable, and the analytics attrition rate should be similar to (or even better than) the business generally.

An analytics head can do plenty to ensure "regretted employee attrition" is minimised, including:

- Many banks have internal employee satisfaction surveys. Ensure they are fairly administered (no prompting or pressuring), study the results, and take corrective actions. If you don't have a survey, start one.

- All similar analyst roles should be aligned *across the organisation*. In nine of ten cases, there will be significant and unjustifiable discrepancies—in the role's description, experience required, and remuneration.

  My day #1 request of HR is always the same: show me all the job descriptions, salary ranges (base and bonus) and external market reference comparisons for all analyst roles across the organisation (include Risk Management and Finance as a minimum start point).

  You may be surprised by the anomalies and inconsistencies. Quickly plug all identified gaps and issues.

- Make sure every role has a clear job description and articulated possible career paths. Some people are remarkably happy to do the same role year after year; but most are not. Keep people moving, learning, and developing.

  I know this sounds obvious, but it requires active effort and it's easy to apply inconsistently.

- Engineer opportunities for everyone to work on something interesting, at least every now and again—think special projects and new initiatives. This is particularly important for the more junior analysts, who often get dumped with the more mundane day-to-day responsibilities.

- Protect the more junior analysts from bullying by more senior clients, from soul-destroying grunt work, and from irrational project demands.

The observation has been made previously and is worth repeating. You cannot expect a junior to say "no" to the head of sales (or anyone senior); set up operational procedures so they don't have to.

Reporting Lines

One of the easiest ways to encumber your analytics function is to get the reporting line wrong. Analytics should not report to Marketing, Finance, Strategy, Risk Management, or Customer Franchise (or any other New Age convenience invented by management consultancies).

Analytics should have the same reporting line as the key client groups (which maybe comprises Marketing, Credit Cards, Lending, Distribution, E-banking, etc). It should probably also be the same reporting line as Risk Management.

The rationale is clear. Analytics must be seen as equal to these groups. The head of analytics should be a peer of the leaders of the client groups. Without this equivalence, it is impossible to affect the necessary organisational transformation; things will just carry on the way they always were.

The last couple of decades have seen the emergence of the CFO and CTO; and more recently we've added the CMO (marketing) and CRO (risk). Well, if you have a CMO, you should definitely have a CAO (analytics). The CAO should not report to the CIO (information) or CDO (data), because they're usually tech focussed. The CAO should probably report to whoever the CMO reports to. Hopefully that clears things up.

The more senior the leader of the analytics function, the more likely you will make meaningful progress on transformation and in extracting business value. Seniority means the search for the right leader becomes more difficult. But that's no reason to compromise your ambition, or indeed the health of your franchise.

Analytics Leadership Skills

I've hired more than a dozen senior analytics leaders in Asia-Pacific. Some roles needed to be transformational. Sometimes a "safe pair of hands" was all that was needed, although that luxury is fast disappearing and transformational analytics is becoming the new business normal—at least in expressed intention.

I don't believe you can appoint generalists for any senior analytics roles. In my experience, seniors need to have "come up through the ranks". The department/functional head must be intimately familiar with business analysis primarily, and much of IIM and advanced analysis also. Time spent in business management can be extremely useful.

Generalists as department heads can manage, but they can't thrive and they certainly won't be transformational, even when they have highly capable one-downs.

The department head remit includes both an evangelical and educational element, which you can't do unless you have absolute confidence in your subject matter. Other business seniors need to understand what is analytically possible, viable and critical. Action plans must then be developed, agreed upon by all stakeholders and managed to completion.

It's straightforward to find individuals with technical skills/experience. But there are other filters dramatically reducing the candidate pool:

- 50% will have sufficient team leadership experience.

- Of that, 25% will have the ability to drive the transformation agenda and interact with seniors.

- Only 5% remaining have done any form of business management. You sometimes have to compromise on this one.

Make sure your succession planning includes rotating the next generation of analytics leadership in business product/distribution roles. The drawback to this approach is that sometimes you won't get them back; but the wider business will be immensely stronger.

CHAPTER 20

Right Place Execution

What does "right place execution" mean? There are two components:

- Focus on the right tasks. It's not uncommon for various operational tasks to become deliverables for the analytics function. Some of these are appropriate, others less so.

- Adopt the right delivery model. Outsourcing is often considered as an alternative to in-house analytics delivery, and many compelling claims are made. Do they stack up?

Focus on the Right Tasks

I've seen an astonishing array of operational activities undertaken by analytics groups. Here are a few examples:

- Activities that "touch" a customer account (maybe a fee adjustment, or a bonus reward payment), utilising the analytics data architecture (warehouses, marts) to determine financial adjustments. The output is normally a file to be uploaded to a front-line operational system to make the physical adjustments.

  Important: Usually, the analytics data architecture is not subjected to the same level of rigorous testing/audit as a front-line operational system. As a result, the build processes sometimes throw up an anomaly or omission, e.g. a data feed is missing from an overnight batch update. This is an inconvenience to analysis; but is business critical when you're dealing with financial adjustments.

There are often economic and operational justifications for using the analytics infrastructure for such activities. If you elect to do so, you need a rigorous and robust project briefing process, and significant compensatory controls—these are relatively high-risk activities. And of course, make sure that the risks are understood by all concerned.

- Updating the Finance Department General Ledger with product operational volumes from the warehouse. There isn't really any excuse for this approach; it's wrong.

- Generating a monthly (or other) data dump for another department to use for customer analysis.

I'm sympathetic to the need, but not the approach. If any department needs to do serious "slice and dice" they should fund dedicated headcount in the analytics group.

I'm not saying all numerically, or analytically, smart people must work in the analytics function—in my experience, they can be the most interesting clients. But centralisation of all analytics activity is vital, particularly as you build out capabilities and coverage.

Remember: standard definitions, consistent analytical rigor, a single source of truth for all reporting, and exploiting scale to better utilise, train and develop analysts.

- Populating data visualisation and business intelligence tools (e.g. Tableau, Qlik, Power BI). There are plenty of vendors out there and some very sexy-looking capabilities. Anyone for real-time tracking of sales by product by branch? Click, click, et viola!

Most of the time the challenge is in accessing the data, particularly real-time or anything close—after all, we're not likely to be running SaaS on a cloud. Fortunately, daily/weekly/monthly is often sufficient.

For dashboards, you can source the basic data from front-line systems. For anything more sophisticated (particularly customer level, rather than product level) you probably need to populate the tools from the warehouse—the single source of truth that will reconcile with other reporting and management information. Such effort might fall to the analytics team; if so, make sure that processes can be automated.

The analytics team will certainly be involved in answering some wide and varied "what does this mean?" queries from end-users. You don't want every member of the analytics team fielding user queries, so get ahead of the curve by ensuring that there's a good data dictionary and a "help line" process (with dedicated resources).

Changing these types of legacy activities can be difficult. There may be some political hot-potatoes, and the rationale for the original allocation of such tasks to analytics might not have disappeared.

In some cases, continuing support for legacy activities is necessary. Others might require an agreed timetable for migration to more appropriate delivery platforms. New requests should be subject to scrutiny with a view to short-term support whilst IT can implement a more appropriate and sustainable solution.

Adopt the Right Delivery Model

Many variations on the analytics delivery model are possible, and outsourcing is an option everyone considers at some point. Enticing claims are made about the benefits of outsourcing, particularly:

- Turnkey solution; fast implementation.

- Scalability, and resource flexibility; "what you need, when you need it".

- Productivity improvements and therefore cost savings.

- Access to scarce and sophisticated analytical resources.

It's not an "all or nothing" choice. Hybrid solutions can be effective, where part of the analytics is outsourced, whilst the rest is delivered in-house.

Let's consider the pros and cons in relation to the different analytics functions described in the last chapter.

Advanced Analytics

Back in 2001, my regional CEO tasked me to "build a team of rocket scientists" to support the advanced analytic needs of a dozen separate country businesses.

Four months later the India Analytics Centre began work on its first projects and I was spending most of my life in Chennai or shuttling around the region trying to generate project work.

The idea was a good one. High end analytical talent was relatively scarce across the region. We'd had initial success in building analytical capabilities in multiple markets, and a Centre of Excellence could accelerate this. We already had good infrastructure to leverage in India, there was plenty of analytical talent, analyst salaries were around 25% of those in mature markets (and 50% of the others), and the India banking leadership team were committed to making our CoE a success.

We were probably the first major bank to adopt this approach, and many have followed.

The continuing popularity for outsourcing advanced projects is easy to understand. For typical projects:

- It's straightforward to identify and ring-fence which data to use.

- The project brief is unambiguous and does not require significant business context knowledge.

- You gain access to advanced talent quickly, with no need for recruitment of internal personnel.

- If demand for advanced projects is relatively low and sporadic, hiring internal expertise may not make practical sense, anyway.

The smaller the organisation, the more attractive the outsourcing solution. But as advanced project volumes rise, the attraction of an in-house solution becomes stronger.

For risk and fraud models a multinational bank can aggregate country level activities to justify the formation of a Centre of Excellence. Local banks usually rely on outsourced expertise; there simply aren't enough different applications to justify a dedicated in-house solution.

For marketing applications, advanced analytical effort is typically applied to improving efficiency, e.g. offer targeting. Implementation often requires quick turnaround, on-the-fly performance tweaks once deployed, and the use of multiple targeting models in combination.

Once more than a few marketing models are in use, it is usually be most effective to deliver in-house.

Business Analysis
Any attempt to outsource the most senior business analysis role is probably a mistake. They are the analytics interface with the business. They should be seen as integral to the businesses they support, and they need to be in close physical proximity to those teams in order to best understand requirements and the business context. Remote support just doesn't work as well.

These are precious resources, with the ability to translate a business problem into analytical action. If you have these resources already, don't lose them. If you don't already have them, develop and nurture them as a matter of urgency.

You might try outsourcing the more junior analyst roles—those with a project delivery function, often to a specification worked up by (or with) the lead business analyst.

I went down this road back in 2003 when we built a Centre of Excellence in Zhuhai, China. The rationale was simple: to exploit the massive difference in salaries between Hong Kong and mainland China by outsourcing the more basic work to the CoE.

Times have changed and it's not an approach I would advocate today. We have better platforms and tools that are driving productivity improvements, and automation can handle most regular (monthly/weekly/daily) reporting. The cost differential holds far less attraction today.

And do you really want to destroy the junior analyst pipeline for succession or expansion of the senior analyst population?

Infrastructure and Information Management
Outsourcing IIM functions in isolation makes no sense, much of the day-to-day activities support analytics delivery and need to be in close proximity to the business analysts (the users) and the IT teams responsible for maintaining the underlying operational data.

If you outsource business analysis, then some aspects of IIM can also be outsourced (provisioning platforms and tools, data management and report automation), whilst others would need to be transferred to the businesses they support (external data acquisition, governance and control)

I've also seen some stand-alone success in outsourcing the build of the data platforms, particularly where you are using proprietary software.

Evaluating Outsourcing Benefits

Earlier we hypothesised four potential benefits from outsourcing. Let's look at each in detail.

Turnkey solution; fast implementation
Any vendor has substantial expertise and experience in building capabilities. They understand how to build data platforms quickly and they have analytical resources that can be swiftly applied.

Their ability to "climb the learning curve" is probably only limited by your own ability to engage.

Scalability, and resource flexibility: "what you need, when you need it"
The capacity to adjust scale quickly holds a particular allure. The analogy of a tap being turned up or down to adjust the flow of analytical support on demand is obviously attractive, particularly if your own organisation is rather less agile. The greater your internal inertia, the louder the siren call.

But think about it from the supply side (the vendor perspective). They want to maximise the return on their analytical talent, and it's actually counterproductive to move analysts between clients—which involves dumping one "mindset" (including business context) and picking up another. And that also assumes that other clients are available to drop/pickup resources in sync with your demand changes. This sounds infeasible, even at scale.

There's definitely implementation *scale up* advantages, particularly in the fast deployment of new resources. For a start-up, this can be attractive. You inherit the operational procedures and practices of the vendor; you need not build for yourself. You exploit their ability to hire and train new talent quickly.

But even in this scenario, when some level of initial maturity is reached, it is useful to assess whether longer-term delivery should be moved in-house.

Productivity enhancements and therefore cost savings
Savings might come from improved productivity (from platforms, tools and working practices). You might also get a cost saving if your supplier is working in a lower cost country. But variations in analyst salaries are much less now; the heady days of 50-75% savings are long gone.

Perhaps the outsource analysts are far superior to those you might have internally. That may be true if you have a small and relatively inexperienced internal team. Otherwise, my experience would suggest it's often the opposite, particularly when you consider knowledge of intimate business and historical context.

So, whilst there might be a cost advantage, it is probably insufficient justification for taking the outsourcing route.

Access to sophisticated analytical resources
For all but the most cutting-edge applications, barriers to pursuing in-house advanced analytics are lower than ever:

-   For most applications analytical talent is more readily available now that at any time previously.

- For most types of analysis, and in most countries, scarcity is not an issue.

- Multiple low-cost and scalable AI/ML cloud solutions are available (including Microsoft, Google, Amazon, IBM, Alibaba).

It's no longer about *access*, it's about *scale*. It's not economically viable for any bank to maintain internal expertise if advanced analytical project volumes are low or sporadic.

If you need to build scale quickly, or if your analytical activity levels are low, then you should consider outsourcing advanced projects. But be careful of the long-term implications.

CHAPTER 21

Governance and Control

Governance and control (G&C) are a critical part of any analytics function—supplying a framework that ensures we perform our work to the best standard, customers are protected from exploitation or data misuse, and the interests and reputation of our employer are not damaged or adversely affected.

There are six components of the governance and control framework for analytics, shown in figure 21.1 below.

Figure 21.1 Governance Framework

Obviously, the analytics function must operate to bank-wide governance standards. The framework here highlights specific risks for analytics—concerning how we manage and access customer data, and how we use it. Policies and controls are required to manage and mitigate those risks.

Data Quality

Consider data quality across two dimensions: adequacy (do we have the right data?) and accuracy (is it correct?).

Adequacy

Periodically review the historical development decisions made about the analytics platforms. This isn't a control concern but represents good data governance. In particular:

- Is the level of coverage (of customers, events, transactions) acceptable?

  Gaps often exist in data, particularly when third parties are used to provide products or services. This can include insurance, mutual funds and rewards redemption, but there are others.

  Is the level of data you are receiving from such suppliers adequate? Does it fully reflect the relationship with the customer? Would more granular information potentially improve understanding and the prediction of customer behaviour?

  Ask similar questions about data gaps that exist with internal systems.

- Is sufficient history of such data being maintained?

  Maybe all data ever available since the first data warehouse was built is accessible. Sometimes, ongoing operational considerations also come into play that might impose storage limits.

  Data on balances (across different accounts and products) should be retained for as long as possible. Transfers to/from the customer and between an individual's accounts should also be given high importance. There's more flexibility with transactional data, particularly merchant payments—they grow voluminous pretty quickly, whilst analytical utility declines. As a minimum keep 24 months of full data, if only to perform YOY comparisons. Determine what is right for the analytical needs (and archive earlier data, just in case).

Updates to operational systems can impact the down-stream analytical data environment. Large changes (like the replacement of a customer service system) are so obvious that any down-stream data warehouse implications are unlikely to be overlooked. But smaller changes can be missed, e.g. the introduction of new products or variants on existing.

Ensure the G&C framework includes explicit responsibility for warehouse updates to the technology teams responsible for maintaining the front-line source systems.

Accuracy

Obviously, we need accurate data. Accuracy should be reflected in the physical data items. Are we looking at the right fields? Are we interpreting things correctly? Does the data reconcile back to the source system?

Some small level of inaccuracy is usually acceptable, e.g. a few missing transactions, or the slight under-reporting of a customer balance. The business implications of such omissions are relatively slight when the warehouse is exclusively used for generating customer communications and performance tracking. But if the warehouse is being used for higher risk activities (say, regulatory reporting, or for financial adjustments to customer accounts) then the impact of errors is significantly higher—and more robust reconciliation processes are required. This was first discussed in Chapter 20.

Either way, controls are needed to monitor business-as-usual (BAU) regular warehouse build and update processes. These should include:

- Did all expected source system feeds get processed?

- Did the processing occur as planned across all components of the extract-transform-load (ETL)?

- Does the updated warehouse accurately reflect the new data? Basic checking (frequency distributions, current versus previous comparisons, etc) will identify obvious errors.

Such controls are the responsibility of the technology team tasked with maintaining the data architecture. Monitoring should be automated, with log files and alerts generated as necessary.

Regular builds will benefit from additional checking by the analytics Information & Infrastructure Management (IIM) team. It provides a further level of comfort. This is easiest done using a set of standard reports, comparing the current period (month, week, day or other) versus prior and flagging anomalies. Much of this can be automated.

Accuracy is also reflected in the timeliness of updates. If customer circumstances have changed since the data was last updated, what are the business impacts of not updating? This is a continually evolving area. Some offers-in-context need real-time recognition; support for APIs may demand elements of real-time data update and analysis.

Update frequency has potential business consequences. Maybe it's imperfect knowledge for decision making; maybe it's missed opportunities. As with data adequacy, periodically review and plan for future need.

Data Dictionary

A data dictionary, as defined in the **IBM** Dictionary of Computing, is a "centralized repository of information about data such as meaning, relationships to other data, origin, usage, and format".

Data dictionaries for analytics warehouses are sometimes rudimentary, maybe a basic list of available tables/fields on the analytics platform and the location of the same data items on a source system.

A fully functional data dictionary should include, for every data item:

- Extract-transform-load (ETL) processes. This is useful to understand how to reconcile the data seen on the warehouse with the same data on its source operational system (analysts do this often).

- Historical data inconsistencies. These may reflect changes in the underlying source data (like system upgrades), changes to product configurations, or something else. Ideally, such inconsistencies are corrected by changes in the ETL to normalize the data.

- Expected values and meanings, e.g. if a gender field has 0 and 1, how should this be interpreted?

- Historical issues log, expanded as new issues are identified.

The data dictionary should be a critical piece of data intelligence, and time should be spent developing and maintaining it—by the IIM team with support for all analysts. A multi-year catch-up program may be required to gradually build out full coverage.

Data Privacy

Data privacy abuses and data leakage reports appear in the media with depressing regularity. Each reminds us we are the custodians of personal and highly sensitive information on customers, their transactions and interactions.

Many jurisdictions have responded with data protection legislation that prescribes what data can be collected, how it should be maintained and used, and consumers' rights (including some options on how the data is used). The EU General Data Protection Regulation (GDPR) currently affords the most comprehensive coverage (reinforced further by some EU member states).

Analytics compliance with local personal data privacy regulation is assumed. There are some further aspects of privacy to be considered, starting with a "wake-up call" relating to staff accounts.

Dealing with Staff Accounts

The handling of staff accounts on any analytical data warehouse can be problematic. Consider four potential approaches:

- Include staff accounts and treat them like any other customer.

  This is sometimes the approach, although the name and other personal data may be masked. It's relatively easy for any moderately determined analyst to identify the salary of other employees. You don't need to know personal data; account numbers will suffice, or open date, age, and gender. All help narrow in on any potential target. Go to lunch with the person, get them to pay, and then search for the transaction. *The vulnerability here is huge.*

- Include staff accounts, but do not include transactional information.

  This is slightly more secure, but only marginally so. It's not too difficult to work out the net change month-on-month or intra-month. It removes the risk from restaurant transactions, though.

- Include staff accounts, with no balance or transactional information.

  There's sufficient information to show product holdings, but volumes, wealth and salary information are unobtainable.

  This can cause issues when trying to reconcile volumes with source operational systems. And what to do, if you're using the warehouse to report balances to your banking regulator? You may need processes to add back the missing information en masse for specific applications.

- Do not include them in any platform build.

  The most secure, and the simplest, but with similar downsides to the previous approach.

Data Classification
Classification should assign different levels of security according to data sensitivity and risk (from disclosure, destruction, or alteration). A simple and effective approach has two levels of data classification: personal and private.

Personal data includes name, ID number (if any) and contact details (including address, phone numbers and emails). The data should not be accessible by the general analyst population, although access is still required in limited circumstances, including:

- To verify data warehouse build correctness by reconciling against operational systems.

- Some customer selections (whether for data mining, reporting, or customer communications) need checking against operational systems.

- Customer communications need contact details, although the process that generates the detail can be mostly automated to reduce risk.

Private data comprises everything held about the customer that isn't personal but is confidential. The general analyst population may access this data.

Data Segregation

Segregation adds another level of access control; and it's a control that can be highly granular and focussed. Segregation ensures that analysts can only access data relevant to their job. Think of it this way: a wealth management analyst doesn't need to see detailed credit card data, and a cards analyst doesn't need to see wealth management data (at least most of the time).

Segregation is managed via *user profiles*. Different profiles allow access to different areas of the data platform (and are restricted from others). Access controls apply to individual tables on a warehouse, or data marts, or even spreadsheets. Figure 21.1 shows a simple example of how it works.

			Credit cards data		***Wealth mgmt data***	
			Personal	**Private**	**Personal**	**Private**
Analyst staff group	**Cards**	Junior	-	✓	-	-
		Senior	✓	✓	-	-
	Wealth	Junior	-	-	-	✓
		Senior	-	-	✓	✓
	IIM	Junior	-	✓	-	✓
		Senior	✓	✓	✓	✓

Figure 21.1 User Profiles

This example has two data domains (credit cards and wealth management), two grades of analyst (junior and senior), and three analyst work groups (credit cards, wealth management, and the information/infrastructure team). There can be more levels of classification, segregation, and analyst work groups.

Data Security

Data security protects against attack—whether by deletion, amendment, corruption, theft, or some other malicious intent.

Some preceding data privacy approaches ensure that analysts only access data that is relevant to their job responsibilities. This also assists data security by limiting opportunities for data theft.

The foregoing discussion of data quality and data privacy considered general guidelines and suggestions. For data security, there are some specific policy recommendations.

Pseudo-account Numbers

Replace all real-world account numbers with pseudo-account numbers that only have meaning within the data warehouse. So, linking a customer (in one warehouse table) to their transactions (in another warehouse table), uses the pseudo-account number, not the customers real-world account number.

It should not be possible to reverse engineer a real-world account number from the pseudo-account number; it must remain unknowable to those with access to the analytics data platform.

Physical Data Movement Policy

Besides data access controls, there should be physical controls.

The analytics function should reside within a restricted area. This offers security and reinforces to all staff (not just analysts) the sensitivity of the data.

The physical movement of data must be controlled. Physical media (e.g. thumb drives) should be locked down, and there should be a size limit on outbound file transfers and email attachments.

But you can't lock out everyone; some access and movement are necessary. All movement requests should be logged (including details of recipient, explanation of the data, the number of records, date extracted, date sent, and expiry date). An *Information Movement Form* can capture the critical details and sign-off for any transfer.

Extracted data must have an expiry date. Data must be destroyed/returned upon expiration. All media/transfers must be encrypted.

Where data is being sent to a third party (say, a print shop), that party must first be vetted to ensure acceptable security standards are in place. Compliance should be audited.

Seed Policy
Seeds are known contacts (usually employees) who are added to communications for monitoring purposes. The primary aim is to protect against the unauthorised use of the data by third parties.

Secondary objectives can include monitoring of:

- The timeliness of delivery
- Completeness of the delivery (mail insertions, email attachments/links)
- Quality of response handling

Mandate seeds for the first few campaigns with any new external vendor. Consider using seeds with all large customer communication supported by an external vendor.

Seeds should monitor all contacts and report back to a *seed co-ordinator*. All reported activities must be reconciled against known solicitations and anomalies investigated as potential data breaches. I've been Albert Haylett, Brian Haylett, Colin Haylett (and so on) for seeding and reconciling communications to precise marketing activities.

List Expiry Policy
This policy should apply to all customer communications, but particularly marketing and sales offers. The policy ensures (a) the freshness and accuracy of the data; (b) timely compliance with changes to a customer's opt-out status; and (c) the limitation of opportunities for data leakage.

Important considerations:

- Determine what the "live" period should be. This should not be longer than one month; but shorter than this may have troublesome process implications.

- The expiry date should be communicated downstream along with the data. External vendors (including bulk emailers, print shops, and fulfilment houses) should be aware of, and in compliance with, the policy.

- Additional processes will probably be required to reflect customer opt-out changes whilst any list is "live".

Execution Integrity

In addition to data integrity, we need to consider approaches that mitigate the risks associated with the three core analytics disciplines: developing predictive models, performing analysis, and generating actions for customer relationship management (CRM) driven activities.

There are a few general policies to consider.

Clean Desk Policy & Secure Waste Destruction Policy
Such policies are typical for a bank and should be rigorously enforced within analytics. This isn't just about customer confidentiality; reports and management information are also commercially sensitive.

Document Retention Policy
Consider extending the retention period for analytics projects. Ensure that all projects are meticulously documented—to provide an audit trail in the event of error, data leakage, or some other enquiry. Documentation should include:

- Description of methodology

- Detailed steps and milestones

- All computer code used (SAS, SQL etc)

- Any intermediate datasets

Modelling

Predictive models have traditionally been subjected to a variety of controls across the model lifecycle. These typically include:

- Guidelines on variable selection (primarily to ensure compliance with anti-discrimination regulation and best practices);

- Development standards (including performance evaluation against a validation sample);

- The monitoring of model operational effectiveness (usually with reference to control groups);

- A periodic review process (to identify redevelopment options and timing).

The oversight is usually formally defined for credit and risk-assessment applications; less so for marketing—reflecting the financial consequences of poorly developed and/or implemented models.

IFRS9 and Basel II/III are driving the use of models for the calculation of expected credit losses[4] (with risk-weighted asset and provisioning implications). In light of this, we can expect regulatory oversight in the use of these models to increase—FRS/OCC SR 11-7 and the ECB TRIM are early examples.

Non-credit/risk activities will probably remain outside the purview of regulators, nevertheless they should continue to be subject to the model life-cycle controls outlined above.

---

[4] The use of predictive tools to estimate probability of default (PD), loss given default (LGD), and exposure at default (EAD). Moving from the "standardised approach" (a portfolio level assessment) towards an "internal ratings based" mechanism (essentially customer level assessment).

Analysis

Any piece of analysis carries risk—that the analysis is wrong and leads to adverse business consequences (financial, reputational, or something else). The greater the risk, the more important the need for mitigation.

Analysts perform accuracy checks at various stages of an analysis.

At a very early stage, the group of customers to be analysed is selected. A sample of customers should be verified against the source system data to ensure the correctness of the selection criteria used—this will catch incorrect inclusions but will not detect erroneous omissions. Note that such system checks will require a specific exemption from some data privacy and security protocols (discussed above).

Back in Chapter 14, "Lifecycle Analytics: Credit Cards", we briefly touched on analytics activities to support spend stimulation programs. Such approaches typically set a goal for the customer (a spend threshold, for example) and a reward for achievement (e.g. entry in a prize draw, or a cash rebate).

The task of assessing which customers achieved the goal often falls to analytics; it represents a high-risk activity because there are financial impacts on customer accounts. Once eligible customers are identified, checking should be done by both analytics and the requesting department—shared responsibility raises understanding of the complexity and risks associated with such programs. For small numbers of customers, check everyone, for larger volumes use a sample. Verification results should form part of the project documentation.

More complicated and higher risk analyses should always adopt a maker-checker approach: one analyst produces the work; another goes through the work stages to verify correctness. Lower risk analyses require a straightforward peer or senior review of results. Maker-checker review results should also be part of the project documentation.

Regular reporting and management information should use verification and maker-checker for the initial production runs. Thereafter, basic "sanity checking" of results should suffice.

Customer Relationship Management

Controls should be much the same as those for analyses, primarily customer verification and maker-checker. With analysis, the designation of riskiness is often highly subjective; with CRM activities it's more transparent, and usually the campaign cost or expected benefit is indicative of relative risk.

Typically, a campaign comprises multiple cells, each with a specific set of selection criteria. Customers should be sampled from each cell for verification.

These approaches should minimise the possibility of high-risk failures.

Compliance Monitoring

Self-assessment

A critical component of compliance monitoring is self-assessment. The self-assessment framework should test compliance with external regulations, internal corporate governance standards, and departmental policies and procedures.

Controls and compliance with those controls is the responsibility of everyone on the team, although a member of the IIM team should be nominated as the *Self-Assessment Co-ordinator*.

Consider each departmental activity and identify:

- Which regulations, governance standards, policies or procedures are applicable?

- What tests should be performed to determine compliance? Sometimes, these may be passive, e.g. one test for compliance with personal data privacy opt-out might be the number of customer complaints of breach.

- How frequently (and exhaustively) to test? There's no need to test everything all the time.

Issue Escalation

When a compliance breach is identified, an issue escalation process should be initiated.

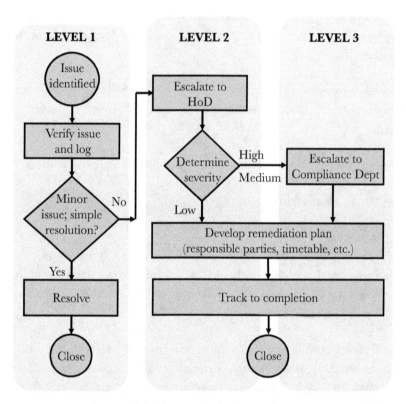

Figure 21.2 Issue Escalation Flow-chart

Figure 21.2 shows one such approach. Use flow-charting to document other analytics procedures (including project initiation and project delivery).

High-Risk Activities

Analytics is sometimes called upon to perform certain high-risk activities including constructing operational data feeds, generating operational reporting and amending customer accounts for monetary adjustment.

All high-risk activities should be subject to additional controls, including significant maker-checker reviews.

Ideally, agreement to execute a new high-risk activity should be for a limited time period only and not exceeding 12 months. The requesting business area should develop a migration plan, covering the transfer of the activity to a more appropriate operational area (or system).

Where such a migration is not feasible or technically possible, senior management should be made aware of the ongoing risk (via the central compliance or operational risk reporting lines).

Periodic Audits

Periodically, the analytics function should be audited—an independent review and assessment of compliance with policies and procedures. The audit might be conducted by internal staff (maybe from another division, country or function), or by an external agency (sometimes specialists, but most often the existing finance or technology auditors).

The best audits won't just test for compliance with controls, they'll also:

- Apply an expert eye to assess whether there are gaps in existing controls, leading to potential vulnerabilities.

- Identify emerging risks that may need addressing within the governance framework.

- Operate pragmatically. Sometimes, it's not a black/white decision about compliance with a specific policy; consideration of compensatory controls and operational context can be necessary.

It's hard to find good analytics practitioners to recruit to your team. It should therefore be no surprise that it's also hard to find good data and analytics auditors. Persevere, since an effective and valued audit partner might be the difference between success and an operational error of significant business impact.

CHAPTER 22

Bloopers

Enough of the successes, the heroic achievements, the brilliant predictive solutions and huge business contributions. Because sometimes it goes a little awry and a wheel falls off.

In this chapter, we will focus on mistakes, errors in development, problems in execution, cockups and screw-ups. The folly, the foolish, the faulty, the failures. There've been a few littered throughout the preceding pages, but here it is our primary theme.

Tragic Targeting

This is from a UK credit card direct response model developed 25 years ago. A junior analyst excitedly delivered his first targeting model. And the most predictive variable was.... (drum roll).... the "customer opt out of marketing" flag.

Key learning:

- His boss really should have had his back

Not the only time I've seen someone left stranded by their boss at a presentation. At a Risk Management conference in Asia ten years ago, the VP of Risk was absent whilst one of the AVPs delivered the results of a project to be the first in Asia to launch a new underwriting system. At the conclusion of the presentation, it was Q&A time.

Question: "What is the key learning from the project?"

Answer: "Don't be a pilot."

Play Carefully with Sharp Knives

Smart tools have enabled terrific improvements in analyst productivity. But dangers are present, particularly when these tools are available to inexperienced analysts. Here's how one scenario played out.

Risk Management had a behaviour score that was getting a little tired and predictiveness was falling. A new version was scheduled for development (by the centralised regional team), but some months away. In the interim, the local Risk team thought they might have a solution.

The result of their effort was a decision tree, a section of which is shown in Figure 22.1. Across all customers, the bad rate (default) was 2.78%; the lower the behaviour score (B-score), the higher the bad rate. From the section of tree shown, any idea what the concern might be?

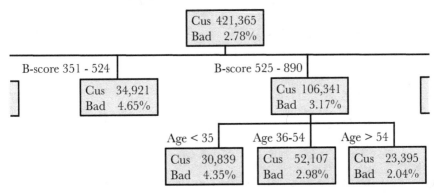

Figure 22.1 B-Score Incorporated in Decision Tree

We don't know how the B-score was constructed, but it is likely to include age, since it's a strong predictor. In the tree, the B-score and age are both used as variables; they're supposed to be independent and clearly aren't. The tree has introduced "multicollinearity", which will skew results and cause volatility. In simple terms, the importance of age is likely being exaggerated.

Key learning: Analytical tools are becoming easy to use, but you still need expertise in development and the subject matter.

Cash Advance Crash and Burn

For background, and in the spirit of full disclosure, I'm not a fan of cash advance promotions. In-depth analysis invariably shows that they cannot be cost-justified.

Look at the target group results in Figure 22.2. All looks as expected for a cash advance promotion. The average cash increases from $68 in the pre-promotional period to $241 during the promo. It then quickly returns to the pre-promotional level.

Average cash	Target	Control
Target volume	5,629	3,247
Pre-period cash	$ 68	$ 51
Promo period cash	$ 241	$ 54
Post period 1	$ 119	$ 49
Post period 2	$ 78	$ 47
Post period 3	$ 69	$ 54

Figure 22.2 Cash Advance Results

As expected, the average cash for the control group (who did not receive the offer) stays broadly flat across all periods under study. But there's a problem. Spotted it?

Yep, the control group exhibits a different behaviour to the target group. The control pre-period average cash level ($51) is 25% lower than the target; they should be the same.

I was blinded by my conviction that the campaign would fail. I didn't spot the control group issues... embarrassingly, the client did.

Key learnings:

- Credibility is precious, don't blow it

- Check that control groups are correct before campaign launch

Mutual Fund Fiasco

Here's another control group problem. This time, the promotion was a mutual fund commission reduction offer delivered by the branch relationship managers to their own customers. Figure 22.3 shows the summary results.

	Target	Control
Customer contacts	3,000	1,500
Response rate	12.70%	10.50%
AUM pre-promo	$319,982	$327,840
Promo uptake	$51,700	$34,070

Figure 22.3 Mutual Fund Promo Results

The problem here is that the response rate for the control group is crazy high. The regular response rates (not shown) across an RM portfolio of customers were typically less than 5%. So, what is going on?

The leads were delivered to the front-line lead management system. As they were being worked RMs noticed some favourite customers were missing... so they called them anyway.

Key learnings:

- The front-line won't miss a golden sales opportunity
- Do your testing somewhere else, then deploy results everywhere

Enthusiastic Amateurs

This promotion was done by one of my in-country teams. It was an anti-attrition offer to those customers most likely to attrite in the next three months. Targets were identified using an anti-attrition scorecard. Two offers were tested.

Offer #1: A rice cooker (value US$50) for spending above US$2,000 from 1st February to 30th March.

Offer #2: A voucher (value US$25) for spending above US$1,000 from 1st February to 31st April.

		Volume	Attrition
Offer #1	Target	500	3.0%
	Control	1,000	3.1%
Offer #2	Target	5,000	2.7%
	Control	5,000	3.0%

Figure 22.4 Anti-attrition Results

Figure 22.4 shows the reported results. Attrition was measured over the subsequent four months. The analyst team made three conclusions. Let's look at each.

Offer #2 is more effective than offer #1
No idea whether this is correct. A comparison is not possible because the duration of the promotion is different, and so is the spend threshold.

Offer #1 is not effective
Possibly not true. The sample size (500 and a 3% response) is small. The volume suggests that the business never really *believed* in the offer (maybe because it was the most expensive).

Offer #2 is most effective and should be adopted ongoing
Probably not true. The attrition saved is tiny (target 2.7% versus control 3.0%) and the economics of continuing are likely poor.

Key learnings:

- This was personally difficult for me. The team was proud of this work, their first real model-based campaign.

- More analyst training was desperately required.

Not So Random Numbers

From time to time, a prize draw (or something similar) will crop up requiring support from the analytics team. You can imagine the kind of thing: "For each transaction you make in June, you get an entry into the Grand Draw." Fulfilment will often fall to the analytics team.

This could have turned out really badly. All subsequent promotions were classified as high risk, with many compensatory controls. I'm not going into the details; the error was caught just in time; and...

Key learning: Remember to randomise the seed for your random number generator. Otherwise, the same numbers will be generated over and over.

The Day I Mailed Mr. Ass

This really did happen. Technical details below have been simplified for brevity.

Let's close out with an oldie-but-goldie. Embarrassingly, this genuinely happened, was 100% my fault and is an early career lesson in the need for accuracy over speed.

It was a small mailing, maybe 10,000 consumer names targeted from a prospect list of around 30,000; no smart targeting, we used selected postcodes/zips using geodemographics.

My mailing addresses had been cleaned, postcode-enhanced, and the geodemographic codes attached. It just needed extraction of the correct geodemographic targets and the final generation of the salutation field. Our production folks could schedule the job for next Tuesday (three work days away). I figured I'd do it myself, but I had to write some code from scratch. The basic steps that I went through are shown below.

Here's the original data:

| J | O | N | A | T | H | A | N | | B | . | | A | B | E | R | C | R | O | M | B | I | E | | A | N | D | | A | S | S | O | C | I | A | T | E | S |

Critically, and foolishly, this was loaded into a 32-byte character array:

| J | O | N | A | T | H | A | N | | B | . | | A | B | E | R | C | R | O | M | B | I | E | | A | N | D | | A | S | S |

Identify the surname by skipping back until whitespace or punctuation:

A	S	S

Find the forename by scanning from the start:

J	O	N	A	T	H	A	N

Generate salutation (gender specific if possible):

D	E	A	R		M	R		A	S	S

In my defence, they were supposed to be consumer names, not businesses. And how many consumer names are over 32 characters long? At least I got the gender correct.

The irony of this story is that we had all kinds of "rude word suppression" algorithms available. It was mostly driven by serious issues with certain major data sources. For example, the UK Electoral Roll had elector names like "The c_ck s_cking b_tch from room 4" (my censorship), often submitted by institutional residences (like care homes). The data capture agents in Sri Lanka just typed what they saw.

At one point, I suggested to my managers that the need to update our "offensive word and phrase database" was desperate. To support my request, I supplied numerous examples of omissions. They agreed, and a bunch of us headed to a hotel offsite location for a whole day of (fully catered) research and brainstorming.

By lunchtime we'd identified several hundred synonyms for male and female body parts, and by day-end we had a few thousand words and phrases for all manner of human activities, bodily functions and interpersonal situations.

It'll be some time until AI can do even half as good a job!

CHAPTER 23

Analytics in a Time of Covid

During the last months of preparing this book—whilst dotting the i's and crossing the t's—Covid-19 hove into view, first as a mild annoyance and later as an epoch-defining tragedy.

Right now (Christmas 2020), we're in transition from the world before the coronavirus to whatever comes next. There remains much uncertainty about what post-Covid might look like and no clear roadmap to take us there.

For analytics and analysts, here are some things to look out for.

Changes in Consumer Behaviour

There have been dramatic changes in consumer behaviour—forced by lockdown restrictions, tightening economic circumstances, and risk avoidance.

Some will right themselves, in full or in part, when recovery comes—we will get back on aeroplanes, we will play team sports, we will go to pubs and restaurants. High Street retailers may claw-back some volumes lost to online players. But some behaviour shifts can never be fully undone or reversed. Covid has hastened online migration and irreversibly changed many behaviours.

There's also been an acceleration of the move to digital banking. Banks with a strong digital offering, particularly those with seamless and speedy new account opening, remittance services and merchant payments, will benefit most in a post-Covid recovery.

But it's unclear what that recovery will mean for different banking products. There has already been drawdown of savings, active searching for credit, and early settlement of outstanding loans (for those that are able). In an uncertain future, do consumers reject instant gratification (the "buy now, pay later" mentality) in favour of more prudent financial management?

> **Much of the data that feeds analytics is no longer valid or appropriate. Segmentations and predictive models of response, product need and expected behaviour are compromised... at best. At worst, they are obsolete.**

Credit/Risk

Changes in consumer circumstances and behaviour have impaired scorecard performance—unsurprising, in a world where "airline pilot" can now be classified as a "risky occupation".

In a rapidly deteriorating credit environment or in times of increasing uncertainty, there is a standard playbook. For most, the immediate response to Covid was to "batten down the hatches" by restricting new credit exposure and limiting contingent liability (with some cutting of open lines).

The next phase is already with us and includes:

- Understanding the underlying market dynamics: segment level loss characteristics, expectations for recovery, etc.

- Reassessing what is an appropriate level of risk (and loss) by segment.

- Adjusting product and customer level business objectives and credit approval criteria to reflect these new perspectives.

- Recognising customer relationships to inform lending (and collections, foreclosure, or rescheduling) decisions.

This must be a continuous exercise, tuning actions as the story unfolds and (hopefully) increasing surety as stability emerges.

I've experienced a few major credit down-turns—all characterised by a swift deterioration of asset quality and an uncertain outlook. On every occasion, the banks that benefited most strongly in recovery did some things better than the pack:

1) They had excellent risk *and* non-risk analytics capabilities.

2) They rode the recovery wave up, continuously undertaking small tests of lending criteria.

3) Once a sustainable recovery was underway, they invested into it; rolling out winners, making plenty of small bets to continue testing, and expecting some might be losers.

> **Data is incomplete and imperfect. Scorecards aren't working. Ongoing detailed performance analysis is vital.**
>
> **Established banks will use judgemental lending approaches. They know their customers. They have historical information on performance, payments and wealth. *They have relationships.***
>
> **Test, test and test again... with robust performance tracking.**
>
> **Leverage learnings and gain "first mover advantage" by investing in the recovery.**

The Analytics Formula for Post-Covid Success

The macro-economic impacts of Covid (depressed GDP, increased unemployment, massive public sector borrowing, etc) will have knock-on implications for banking in the longer term.

Even markets that survive Covid *relatively* well will not fully escape the global ramifications.

We should expect:

- Higher bad loans, generally higher levels of consumer risk, and the need for robust credit application decisioning and ongoing customer exposure management.

  Analytical support will be required for:

  a) More testing and monitoring.

  b) Redevelopment (or recalibration) of loss prediction mechanics.

- Increased competition for "good" customers (whether for assets, or for the liabilities to fund them). Analytics needs to be applied to:

a) Smart acquisition targeting.

b) Existing customer cross- and up-sell (and particularly diversification into fee generating products). These customer bases must be worked hard.

> **Analytical bench-strength will determine which banks adapt best to the post-Covid environment... and deliver the best customer and shareholder value.**

The Covid Discontinuity

As discussed, our predictive mechanisms are either compromised or broken. We need new, stable data to rebuild our understanding; and that will take time, probably multiple years.

When we eventually reach a stable post-Covid state, and we look backward through time, there will be a period of significant volatility... marking the transition from the pre-Covid world.

Every piece of atomic data, every piece of MI, every backward-looking report... there will be a discontinuity. The smooth trend lines will be broken by turbulence induced by Covid.

This *Covid Discontinuity* will eventually fade into the rear-view mirror and become less and less important in performance evaluation. But remember, when we review mortgage losses and early redemptions, we are sometimes looking at up to 30 years of performance; so that Covid wrinkle will take a while to work through.

And for those of us who have lived through it...

we will be reminded of who we lost.

Afterword

Whether you cherry-picked your way through or read every word, here you are at the end. Thank you for your time and attention; I hope you feel it was well spent.

This book started as a training course for a bank in Jakarta, and it just kept growing. Eventually a line was drawn and scope expansion ended—I am acutely aware of omissions and areas of relative brevity.

The hardest part was trying to find the right balance between strategy, theory, and practice. It was important to me that each received adequate coverage, and that the book was accessible and useful to multiple audiences—including CEOs, business managers, and analysts.

I'm advocating a strategy that exploits the rich legacy advantages most banks possess. Analytics should *primarily* be:

- Unlocking the value in the existing customer base through improved personalisation and engagement—and importantly, identifying and fulfilling customer needs (for solutions, products, and services).

- Delivering a fully integrated customer experience across all channels—in communications and the recognition of interactions, transactions, and activities.

If I have moved you to accelerate building analytics capabilities, then I'll count that as a success... and hopefully one less casualty of the new banking paradigm.

Be in no doubt, there will be winners and losers as the pace of innovation quickens. I hope I've improved your chances of being on the right side.

Don't just survive... thrive!

APPENDIX A: Sample Cards Segmentation

Advanced analytics is often applied to growing credit card balances. Typical offers include balance transfer (BT), credit card checks, and instalment loans within the card line.

With any balance development offers, the first stage is to screen customers to establish eligibility. Figure A.1 graphically shows the typical results.

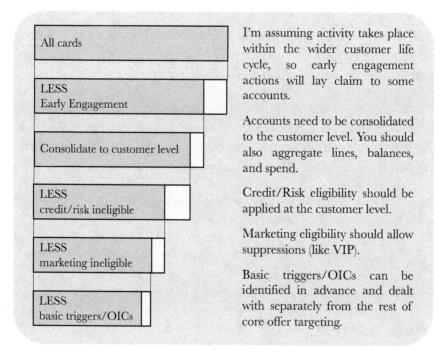

I'm assuming activity takes place within the wider customer life cycle, so early engagement actions will lay claim to some accounts.

Accounts need to be consolidated to the customer level. You should also aggregate lines, balances, and spend.

Credit/Risk eligibility should be applied at the customer level.

Marketing eligibility should allow suppressions (like VIP).

Basic triggers/OICs can be identified in advance and dealt with separately from the rest of core offer targeting.

Figure A.1 Eligibility Waterfall

Triggers and OICs should deliver higher response than core campaigns. Simple examples might include:

- BT term -2 months
- BT term -1 month
- BT out resolicit at +5 months

- Large drop in revolving balance
- Large change in payment ratio
- Relentless balance paydown

The various screening criteria have a significant impact on the volume of customers available to receive offers. The application of additional targeting criteria further restricts volumes.

When using advanced analytics for targeting, we reduce target volumes to increase responsiveness. But continuously targeting the same customers month after month leads to an inevitable plunge in response—the impact of contact fatigue (discussed in Chapter 18). This can be avoided by explicitly recognising fatigue impacts within the model (which has significant implications for the model building process), or in the target selection process.

Another solution is to expand the target population, whilst ensuring all offers are sustainable and economically viable (e.g. profitable). We can do this using segmentation, as detailed in Figure A.2.

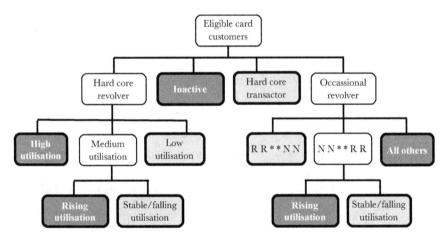

Figure A.2 Credit Card Segmentation

The graphic shows ten target segments (the shading will become obvious as we progress; light means definitely target; dark means maybe not). Let's consider the treatment of each target segment.

Inactive. These customers have been inactive for at least six months. As we learnt in the discussion of attrition, it is hard to reverse this behaviour; any reactivation tends to be brief; profitable behaviour change is elusive.

Leave them alone and build triggers and OICs to target early adverse behaviours that might lead to inactivity. If they become active again, they'll be picked up in another target segment.

Hard core transactors. This group is often low scoring with any modelled targeting; they are therefore mostly excluded from balance development offers. It usually represents a significant volume of potential targets.

One approach is to build targeting analytics specifically for this segment. You may get a viable x3 performance lift from model targeting 15% of the transactor base. So, if these transactors are 50% of the eligible customers, you've expanded the universe by 7.5% (newly targeted customers).

Hopefully x3 lift is sufficient to target offers profitably. Don't bother with price testing; hit them with the lowest price available from the outset; instalment loans usually work better than BT.

Hard core revolvers. These customers revolve 5 or 6 months from 6, but they do exhibit different levels of utilisation. This broad segment breaks out into three subsegments and four targets.

High utilisation. Why would we make any offer? These customers are our most profitable, and they have limited unused lines. Leave them alone. All potential "no offer" segments are shaded dark in the graphic.

Low utilisation. Definite opportunities here; but price relatively high.

Medium utilisation. If the utilisation is rising, then leave them alone; this is profitable behaviour and at regular (non-promo) interest rates. If the utilisation is stable or falling, it might signal opportunities to build balances at medium price points.

Occasional revolvers. Many occasional revolvers will bounce between different states, and they may well end up in a segment discussed above.

The convention used in Figure A.2 is to represent each of the last six months by a single character (R = revolve, N = no revolve, * = either). The RR**NN segment represents customers who were revolving but have not done so for at least the last two months. Make them a reasonably attractive offer, but not at the lowest price.

The NN**RR segment represents customers who have started to revolve. If the utilisation is rising, leave them alone. If it's stable or falling, try to build balances at a medium price point.

The final segment is "All Others", occasional revolvers that don't fit into the other two categories. It covers many behaviours, some more akin to revolving, some closer to transactors. I'm always tempted to leave them and wait until they settle into a more identifiable behaviour. But I've never had the luxury of accumulated sufficient performance evidence for or against this approach. If you want the balances and the revenue early, then spend the money to acquire them. If not, leave for natural development or migration to a more highly actionable segment.

Whatever you do in any of the target segments, make sure you test pricing and a "no offer" control—at least until you have developed a clear plan of segment level actions.

The temptation for business owners may be to maximise the volumes as soon as possible; leaving segments to mature naturally is therefore difficult. But the economics of doing so is easy to measure and the results compelling.

Customers will naturally migrate between different segments. One beauty of this approach is that we are automatically adjusting our treatment (and price) to reflect the changing circumstances.

And don't forget, this activity is augmented by both triggers and offers-in-context to drive more targeted and immediate actions.

APPENDIX B: Contact Protocols

A contact protocol seeks to manage the number of sales and marketing offers each customer receives by channel. Rules are applied at two levels:

- *Customer.* There are usually clearly identifiable and distinct customer bases within any retail bank (initially discussed in Chapter 10 under the cross-sell framework)—let's call these *major products*. For a customer with more than one major product (maybe credit cards, general banking, and mortgage) there needs to be a recognition of the total contacts/offers.

- *Major product.* Where a customer has multiple relationships, a single relationship should not dominate. It therefore requires product level limits. If the customer has a single major product, the product protocols apply (not the customer protocol). For protocol purposes, there should only be a few major products.

There needs to be flexibility in the application of contact rules. Circumstances change and opportunities arise. It would be foolish for us to limit our ability to react to these new events. Therefore, there needs to be recognition and a separate treatment of high priority contact opportunities.

Typically, such high priorities will be highly time-constrained offers-in-context (e.g. the customer walks into a store, or fires up the bank app).

Figure B.1 shows a sophisticated protocol addressing the issues raised in the foregoing discussion.

For almost every incumbent bank, the technical functionality to implement such a protocol is not in place. Though this is based on a real-world application, a few elements were not implemented (and even today remain aspirational).

Do not despair. Consider what is possible and start with a protocol addressing the 30-day rules.

Channel contact maximums		1-day rule	7-day rule	30-day rule
Customer	In-bound	1	2	3
	Direct mail	1	2	3
	Email	1	2	3
	SMS	1	2	3
	App notification	2	3	4
	Telemarketing	1	1	2
Major product	In-bound	1	2	2
	Direct mail	1	2	2
	Email	1	2	2
	SMS	1	2	2
	App notification	2	2	3
	Telemarketing	1	1	1
Priority	In-bound	1	1	2
	Direct mail	1	1	2
	Email	1	2	4
	SMS	1	2	4
	App notification	2	4	4
	Telemarketing	1	1	2

Figure B.1 Multi-product Contact Protocol

Priority contacts are incremental to the customer level limits. Top priority offers need to be gated via an agreed process. Otherwise, there's a danger every communication is designated a priority.

I'm not going into the details of this protocol. The more you consider it, the more you will see the subtlety derived from the mechanics. You may disagree with the thresholds set; this is not intended to be prescriptive. What it should illustrate is the power and precision that is possible when contact protocols are implemented.

LIST OF FIGURES